POST WAR
INDEPENDENT
MOTORCYCLE
FRAMEMAKERS

POST WAR
INDEPENDENT
MOTORCYCLE
FRAMEMAKERS

Keith Noakes

OSPREY
AUTOMOTIVE

First published in Great Britain in 1995
by Osprey, an imprint of Reed Consumer Books Limited,
Michelin House, 81 Fulham Road, London SW3 6RB and
Auckland, Melbourne, Singapore and Toronto.

ISBN 1 85532 531 4

Project Editor Shaun Barrington
Editor Ian Penberthy
Page design Gwyn Lewis

Typeset by Dorchester Typesetting Group Ltd, Dorchester
Printed in Italy by G Canale & C.SpA-Borgaro T.se-Turin

Title page: A 1992 Harris Magnum 4, 1992,
with Suzuki engine. (*Photo Graeme Bell*)

Acknowledgements

I would like to thank the persons and companies, listed here,
for their invaluable help during the writing of this book.

Bimota · Steve and Lester Harris · Bob Stevenson
of Spondon Engineering · Colin Seeley · Dave Degens of
Dresda Autos · Nico Bakker · Fritz Egli · Richard Peckett
of P & M Motorcycles · Ron Williams of Maxton · Segali
Corsa · Derek Chittenden of Hejira · Larry Webb of P D Q
Developments · Malcolm Newell of Quasar · Derek and
Don Rickman · Ken Sprayson · Magni

Plus a special thanks to Roy Jackson, my very patient, and
long-suffering, typist. Thanks also to Roland Brown, Oli
Tennent, Phil Masters, Graeme Bell and EMAP for
additional photographs.

Contents

Foreword

From the beginning of motorcycle sport riders have strived to improve performance and the rider is the best judge of what is required to improve that performance. Of course, in many cases the lack of power from the engine is the problem, but in many cases ample power is available but cannot be used to the full because of bad handling.

To overcome these handling problems many riders carried out modifications to the frame or chassis and, in some cases, completely new frames were built. In the early post war years when the motorcycle factories were only just getting back into operation, development programmes to produce competition motorcycles were rare, so more and more home built frames began to appear. Some of these home built frames were so successful that the riders or builders began to make frames for those who didn't have the ability to do it for themselves. Thus the independent motorcycle frame maker became a good potential business area.

As the larger well-known factories began to produce more over-the-counter racing motorcycles, competition grew fiercer and the quest for better performance got stronger; the situation became more obvious when the Japanese motorcycle industry began to take hold. The Japanese have always used success in competition to enhance their road bike sales, so they soon began to produce over the counter competition machinery and factory race teams to support these sales. I well remember a race meeting at Brands Hatch in 1974: after practice we had a fairly serious steering problem with the aircooled KR 750 Kawasaki and not being spoilt by a multitude of setting parts as is the modern trend, the only way was to hacksaw the head stock out, reposition it and bronze weld it back in. I finished the job at two in the morning. Luckily for me, I concentrated on the riding and not on chassis development, as the result on this occasion did not warrant the midnight oil burnt!

In many cases the engine development was ahead of chassis design and, before long some of these engines were to be housed in frames produced by the small independent frame makers. This process accelerated when some Japanese factory racers began to use frames built by some of the now well known, independent frame makers, who by this stage were the experts. This resulted in more frame making business being established. These independents extended their business by the production of road going machines, in fact many independent frame making companies throughout the world now produce a wide range of exotic road bikes as their main business.

There is no doubt that the independent frame makers have made a major contribution to the development of motorcycle frames or chassis. This book sets out to tell the story of the people and the companies that have, and are still, making a significant contribution to motorcycle frame design.

Mick Grant

■■■■■■ Introduction

Since World War 2 many clever engineers and enthusiasts – and some not so clever – have designed and built motorcycle frames or chassis. These frames were built for personal and specialized use, that is road transport and competition. The latter includes trials, motocross, record breaking and, of course, road racing. Some were built with little thought for their design, so success was not always forthcoming.

All these frames were built for one or two main reasons. First of all, in the early post-war years, the urge to go racing or compete in some form of motorcycle event was often frustrated because suitable machinery was not available, or because what was available was outdated. Secondly, as has always been the case, competition bred an extremely strong urge to gain some technical advantage which, hopefully, would lead to a performance advantage.

Many very clever designers surfaced during this period, but often excellent frames evolved from a combination of engineering skills and an intimate knowledge of what was required. This resulted in the modification of existing machinery until the desired design performance was achieved.

Apart from the many excellent frames to emerge during this period – from one-offs to limited production runs – there were many cases where the builders' natural engineering skills were utilized in the formation of businesses to take full commercial advantage of the potential market for their products. These businesses are the independent frame makers described in this book.

Some of those covered no longer trade, but are included because of their contribution to the progress of the independent frame making business. However, this is also the record of some of those who have been successful, and those who are still designing and building exciting motorcycles utilizing engines from the mainstream manufacturers.

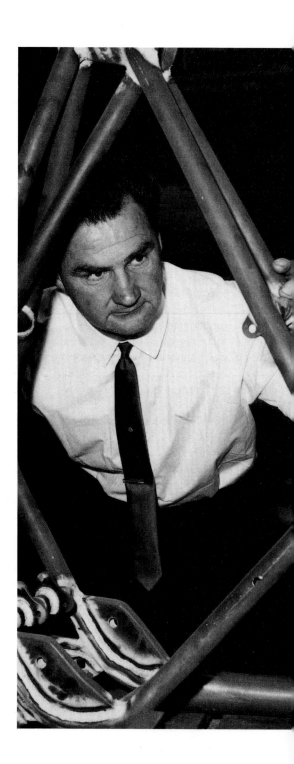

■■■■■ *A unique contribution*

No book on motorcycle frame making could be written without mention of Ken Sprayson, or rather Reynolds, the tubing manufacturers, and Ken Sprayson. Reynolds had been a major source of the steel tubing utilized in the manufacture of motorcycle frames from the early 1900s, but in the immediate post-war years they also undertook the design and production of motorcycle frames. In addition to supplying the steel tubing, Reynolds were also experts in the use of the material. This expertise was passed on to many new frame makers in the United Kingdom and overseas via Ken Sprayson.

During World War 2, Reynolds Tube Co. had gained much experience in the manufacture and use of their high-quality steel tubing in the aircraft industry. After the war they began to look for alternative outlets for their expertise due to the obvious decline in aircraft requirements. During the early 1950s, this expertise found a place in the manufacture of welded motorcycle frames. With their expert knowledge of bending and welding the tubing, they often built pre-production frames for the major motorcycle manufacturers in their own factory.

The first, and very significant, frame contract undertaken by Reynolds was the now-famous Norton featherbed frame. All featherbeds were made by Reynolds after Rex McCandless made the first six in 1950. After the featherbed, Reynolds made the Commando frames before N V T had them made in Italy. Even then, Reynolds were involved in rectifying the Italian-made frames.

Other firms to take advantage of the tubing maker's expertise were B S A and Ariel, for whom Reynolds built their trials frames. In the boom years of the 1950s, Reynolds also built welded frames for many of the post-war motorcycle manufacturers, including Ambassador, Excelsior, Dayton, Douglas, D K W, Tandon, Velocette, A J S, Vernon, D K R and Enfield. Some were in the early stages of setting themselves up to become the independent frame makers described in this book. Among them were Seeley and Rickman, two of the earliest independent frame makers.

Reynolds continued to offer their excellent service until the early 1980s. Throughout this period of the company's history, Ken Sprayson was their expert in the use of their specialized steel tubes. He passed on his welding skills to many, some of whom became well-known frame makers in their own right. To this day, many declare that Ken Sprayson played an important part in their beginnings.

Ken Sprayson may have been the welding expert to whom many turned for guidance, but this skill was only one of his abilities. During the time he was with Reynolds, he was also responsible for the design and construction of many specials, that is competition frames to suit a range of engines for a variety of formulae. During the 1950s, many famous riders were to take advantage of Ken Sprayson's skills, among them Jeff Smith, Geoff Duke, Mike Hailwood and John Surtees.

Although Reynolds closed their welded assembly business in 1981, Ken Sprayson maintained his involvement with motorcycle design and manufacture, and this included spending a few years with BSA. Today, many of the great independent motorcycle frame makers acknowledge their debt to him for the time in the early post-war years when he imparted his talents to many as a new, growing industry was getting underway.

Ken Sprayson; his knowledge and welding skills were instrumental in helping many budding motorcycle frame makers to turn their ideas into reality.

▌▌▌▌▌▌ Nico Bakker

By the early 1970s, Nico Bakker, a very accomplished motorcycle road racer, had reached a point in his racing career where his ultimate performance on the race track was being restricted by the machinery he was riding. However, this was not due, as in many cases, to a lack of power or engine unreliability. Nico had the right engines, and his racing performance demonstrated his riding ability. The restriction lay in the quality of his machine's handling. This is the point where the Nico Bakker story really starts. Although it was purely a private venture, he decided to build a racing motorcycle frame for his own use.

This first Bakker frame was built to very high standards, using only the very best materials. The high quality was to become a Nico Bakker trademark, and it has led to a lasting reputation for excellence and finish. That first frame also proved to be the starting point for a new business, as the very marked improvement in Nico Bakker's race results with this new home-built frame was noted by the motorcycle racing fraternity. It wasn't very

long before requests from other private owners for purpose-built frames began to reach Nico.

The very first commercial frame produced by Nico Bakker was for someone who was to become famous in motorcycle racing. Nico was asked to build a frame to house a 250 cc Yamaha racing engine for fellow countryman Wil Hartog. This was during 1974, the year which can be considered the true commercial starting point for Nico Bakker.

At the beginning of his frame-building career, Nico constructed his frames from steel tubing in the traditional manner, but his racing experience gave him the knowledge of exactly where to put the various tubes to achieve the optimum performance

Above right A typical Nico Bakker frame, complete with swinging rear fork. It is fabricated from aluminium extrusions. This particular example is a 125 cc race frame, of the type used by Peter Ottl.

Below A 1982 Bakker race frame, built to house Yamaha 250 and 350 cc engines.

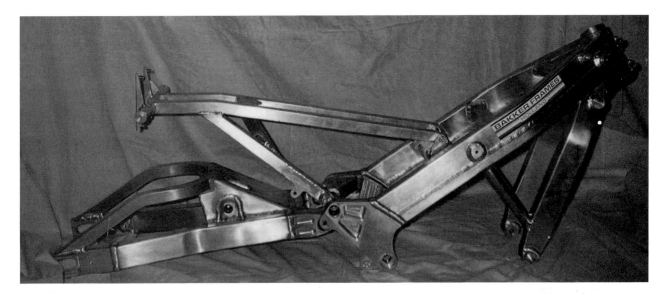

from the frame he was building. This quality of design was matched by the use of the best materials, which soon produced frames that were in demand. Nico was not slow to meet that demand.

By the mid- to late-1970s, Nico Bakker was producing frames for a wide range of engines, from 50 to 1000 cc and in many different forms. In fact, his versatility was such that almost any engine was eligible for the Nico Bakker treatment, and his list of customers was growing continually. It included some very well-known, top-class riders, such as Phil Read, Cecotto, Agostini, Kork Ballington, Jack Middelburg and many others. The comparatively short time in which this demand was achieved is an indication of the admiration that Bakker machines commanded from the motorcycle racing fraternity.

Among the frames designed and built during this period was one to house a 125 cc Morbidelli racer. Like many others produced by Nico Bakker, this frame could be purchased as a kit into which all the original parts would fit, enabling the customer simply to rebuild his own machine into the high-performance frame.

Another engine catered for was the Suzuki 1000 cc. The frame for this engine was a further indication of Nico Bakker's versatility, as it could be offered in road or race trim. The main difference was that the race version utilized a monoshock suspension system, as indeed did the little Morbidelli frame. The 1000 frame was also available in versions to accept Honda 750 and 950 cc engines,

Kawasaki 900 and 1000 cc units, and Suzuki 750 and 1100 cc powerplants.

Also popular and successful during this period was a frame for the famous Yamaha TZ. When supplied as a kit, the frame would accommodate all original 250 or 350 parts. In addition, all the other parts such as petrol tanks, fully-tuned exhaust systems, fairings, seats and wheels were – and still are – produced by Nico Bakker to his usual high standard.

This line of frame design, that is the high-quality, steel-tubing type, continued into the 1980s. Where the engines remained popular or competitive, Nico continued to supply the relevant frames. For example, the ever-popular Yamaha TZ frame was still being produced, but in typical Bakker fashion, it included detail modifications in an effort to optimize the performance. This particular frame would still accept the 250 or 350 cc versions of the engine, and it could still be purchased as a completed machine or in kit form. The 1000 frame was also still available to house a range of engines, and examples such as the Suzuki 1000 cc and the Kawasaki 1000 or 1100 cc engined machines were offered in race or street-legal forms.

Another popular model from the Bakker works at this time was a street-legal frame for the Honda 6 CYL. Other frames to come from this prolific builder included race frames to house a Cagiva 500 cc engine and a Rotax 250 cc engine. The latter incorporated an interesting feature for this period.

It not only had a monoshock suspension, but also the shock absorber was mounted in a horizontal position under the engine's crankcase. This was indicative of Nico Bakker's continual striving for technical improvement.

His desire to improve his products was demonstrated during the mid-to-late 1980s, when he began to use aluminium in his frame designs. The use of aluminium was extended to swinging rear forks. Both frames and forks utilized pre-formed aluminium extrusions and tubes. Considerable modification of the extrusion was often required, along with varying degrees of aluminium fabrication to achieve the required result. This would depend on the style or design of the frame or rear fork. The use of extrusions was ideally suited to the construction of the widely-used, twin-spar type frame, which was – and still is – a very popular frame style suitable for many engine configurations.

Nico took to the use of aluminium as a frame

material in the same professional manner that he did with steel tubing frames. He chose the very best quality materials, and aimed for a very high standard of construction and finish. During the latter half of the 1980s, the fabricated aluminium frame became the standard method of construction in the Bakker factory.

From the very beginning of his business to the present day, Nico Bakker has always been prepared to design and build one-off or short-run examples of his frames to house almost any type or make of engine. However, he has always had a range of catalogued models that have become popular and, therefore, created a demand. This range of standard frames includes both race and road examples. In most cases, these can be supplied as finished machines or as frame kits.

At the time of writing, the Bakker range includes a completed twin-spar frame and swinging rear fork in aluminium to house 125 cc engines, that is a

Left The BMW-based Kangaroo. It utilizes the R100GS air-cooled boxer engine, along with the BMW gearbox and shaft drive.

Above This aluminium twin-spar Formula 1 frame will accept a range of engines, including Suzuki, Kawasaki, Honda and Yamaha, with capacities ranging from 750 to 1100 cc. Note the use of the standard Nico Bakker single-leg rear suspension.

Right This aluminium twin-spar frame houses a BMW K100 engine. The four-cylinder, water-cooled powerplant retains the factory gearbox and shaft drive. It is designated the K100 Special.

full-race-spec. frame. In contrast is the Special Formula 1 design. This is a fabricated twin-spar frame that can be supplied with, or to house, engines from Suzuki, Kawasaki, Honda and Yamaha, in capacities from 750 to 1100 cc. In effect, it is a whole range of machines in one design, but this particular design has something that renders it extra special: it supports a single-leg rear suspension in place of a conventional swinging rear fork.

The single leg is of Nico Bakker design and manufacture, and it is fabricated from aluminium extrusions. This feature does make the machine unique in the motorcycle marketplace. What is even more unique, however, is that the extremely clever design can be sold as a separate unit with leg transmission,

damper, brake, special wheel and mudguard to fit most frames from 250 to 1100 cc.

Another very exciting machine from the Bakker range is the BMW Kangaroo, which is based on the BMW R100GS Boxer. This air-cooled, flat-twin engine, complete with factory shaft drive, is housed in a fabricated, aluminium twin-spar frame, which is welded to swinging rear fork pivot mounts that are machined from the solid. Square-section alloy tubes run under the engine in normal cradle fashion, while the rear suspension is designed to accommodate the standard shaft-drive unit.

Upside-down White Power front forks take care of the steering and handling. The stopping is handled by two Brembo 300 mm (12 in) floating discs and four-piston calipers at the front, and the BMW disc of the rear. Running on 43 cm (17 in) wheels, all this makes an incredible street-legal machine, which is wrapped up in very distinctive and stylish aluminium body panels, or fibreglass panels for those wishing to save some of the cost.

An independent professional rider reported the BMW-based Bakker as being an excellent handling road-going machine, the engine having good torque and producing a claimed top speed of 201 kph (125 mph). Its appeal to the motorcyling fraternity is demonstrated by the speed with which the first ten were snapped up, resulting in a much larger batch being put into production.

BMW engine lovers are well catered for by Nico Bakker, as he catalogues a second machine utilizing an engine from this manufacturer. Again, the frame is a fabricated aluminium, twin-spar type with upside-down White Power front forks. It uses a Brembo four-piston front caliper, while the rear is standard BMW and runs on a 46 cm (18 in) wheel. A 41 cm (16 in) wheel is used at the front. Housed in this frame is the BMW K100 engine, a water-cooled flat-four.

The complete machine weighs in at 188 kg (414 lb), which is 3 kg (7 lb) heavier than the Kangaroo, but this is due to the larger engine and the addition of the cooling system. This very impressive street-legal machine is encased in stylish GRP bodywork. Designated the Nico Bakker BMW K100 Special, it has a tested top speed of 386 kph (240 mph). For those who favour the BMW engine, this machine does full justice to the powerplant, and gives the lucky owner an eye-catching piece of equipment with performance to match.

As this account shows, from the very beginning Nico Bakker has been extremely versatile and has introduced an immense range of technical advances, but his current masterpiece has crowned these achievements. It is a crowd-stopper in appearance, and it offers performance to befit a machine that has received Nico Bakker's attention.

This latest creation is the QCS (quick-change system). It is a unique machine that boasts hub-centre steering and the Bakker single-leg rear suspension. These two features make for easy removal of the single-side-mounted wheels, and resulted in the QCS designation.

Although the ability to change wheels quickly and simply is always a great asset, to assume that this feature is the reason for the design is a mistake. The QCS offers so much technical innovation that its designation under-describes the end product.

The machine was designed to overcome the technical disadvantages of conventional motorcycle design and, therefore, lead to improved performance. Such improvements were considered to be equally important to street-legal machines as road-race versions.

The use of the hub-centre steering layout results in constant steering geometry and wheelbase measurement. These two major points can never be achieved with even the best conventional front fork layout. The QCS layout also allows quicker and easier suspension adjustments, which are major advantages for road-race machines.

The whole design of the QCS is a departure from conventional frame design. Apart from the hub-centre steering and single-leg rear suspension, another major difference is that the engine itself forms a stressed member of the frame.

Although hub-centre steering is not new, Nico Bakker has designed his version of the system to take full advantage of the technical possibilities it offers. This remarkable design utilizes axial pivot steering, which means that the kingpin (formerly the front fork) angle remains constant during suspension movement, resulting in little or no trail change. The result is a machine with much more neutral handling.

Due to Bakker's own six-piston caliper design, braking equal to a twin-disc set-up is achieved using a single ventilated disc. This means a saving in weight, but more importantly, the central position of the single disc in the front wheel means that the gyroscopic effect has a less negative influence on roadholding. The single disc has a unique cooling system, air being forced through a cleverly-designed hollow front mudguard onto the ventilated disc. The rear brake is a twin-piston Brembo caliper.

All this sounds like a very formidable package to be ridden by experts only, but this is not the case. In fact, the machine is claimed to be much simpler to ride than motorcycles of conventional layout. Road test reports by professional riders describe it as being a joy to ride, in terms of comfort and out-

Above Another Nico Bakker first: a six-piston front brake caliper, shown fitted to a QCS.

Left The exciting QCS, minus its bodywork. Note the hub-centre steering and single-leg rear suspension. The engine is used as a stressed member of the frame, the front and rear sub-frames being bolted directly to it.

Above right A QCS finished in street trim. This one is based on a Honda 750 cc engine.

right handling. They remark on the high degree of road feel, something reported as lacking in other hub-centre steering designs, while another notable point is the lack of road shock felt through the handlebars. As there are no forks for mounting the clip-on bars, Nico has utilized a machined alloy plate on a short headstock running on roller bearings. Attaching the clip-ons to this gives the overall appearance of normal handlebars.

The positive feel and lack of road shock are due

Above Another road-going Q C S, but this time with a Yamaha engine.

Above right The most recent of Nico Bakker's projects: the exciting B M W-based Bomber, which makes use of components from the R I I 0 0 R S.

to the unique front suspension and steering arrangement. The front suspension is connected to a front sub-frame at the mounting points, which means that the forces are not concentrated at one point, as is the case with the steering head of conventional front forks. Another advantage of this system is that none of the suspension movement is transmitted to the handlebars. All this improves rider comfort which, in turn, reduces fatigue, and that is of prime importance to long-distance road riders and endurance racers.

All the technological development was carried out on the Bakker prototype, which had the Q C S system built around a Honda R V F 750. However, the production road version utilizes the Yamaha F Z R 1000.

The machine is enclosed by beautifully-styled bodywork and finished to the same very high standard as the rest of Bakker's products. The outstanding bodywork was designed to optimize aerodynamics and rider comfort, the person responsible for this part of the project being Cees Smit, who works with Nico in North Holland.

One interesting and significant fact about the Bakker Q C S machine is that it weighs-in at approximately 10 per cent less than the original Yamaha from which the engine is taken. However, of greater interest to motorcycling enthusiasts is the fact that the Bakker Q C S is not only available for 750 and 1000 cc four-stroke road and race engines, but also for 250 and 500 cc road racing engines.

As well as his extensive range of well-tried and proven designs, at the time of writing Nico Bakker

has just put into production another of his exciting designs. This totally new machine is built around the BMW Boxer engine, as used in the R1100RS. This engine is a fuel-injected, eight-valve version that produces 90 bhp at 7250 rpm.

Having acted as consultant to BMW on the development of their telelever front suspension, Bakker was given their support in the design and production of a high-performance, road-going sports machine. This new design, known as the Bomber, utilizes the engine as a fully-stressed member, the front end of the frame consisting of an alloy box section bolted directly to the engine and carrying the suspension. The rear suspension is a single side swing arm that encloses the driveshaft.

The telelever front suspension is based on a single pivoting wishbone, which operates a suspension unit mounted behind the steering head. This type of suspension is claimed to maintain a higher degree of steering geometry under braking and cornering than conventional forks. Nico has designed the front suspension to produce a ride height that enhances the handling necessary on a sports bike of this calibre, while maintaining the overall appearance of conventional forks.

As with the front end, the rear alloy tubular

sub-frame is bolted directly to the engine and gear-box unit. It carries a carbon fibre seat. The BMW five-speed gearbox takes care of the drive, while the wheels are as used on the R1100RS. The brakes (ABS being an option), instruments, electronics (including the Bosch engine management system), exhaust and lights are all standard R1100RS items. Fuel is carried in a Bakker 22 litre (5 gal) alloy tank, which is beautifully styled, along with the rest of the Bakker bodywork.

This elegant and modern design weighs in dry at 202 kg (445 lb), and is a true sports bike, having an estimated top speed of 222 kph (138 mph).

Dozens of Bakkers

This brief account of the work of Nico Bakker clearly demonstrates the diversity and innovation shown by the frame maker. The sheer number of designs, coupled with the vast range of engines catered for, is impressive. In some cases, consider-able numbers of some designs have been produced by the Bakker factory, illustrating that Nico Bakker can not only produce very advanced designs, but also put them into production.

In addition to supplying completed machines and frames for customers to build their own, Bakker also produces specialized components that can be utilized to enhance the performance of a customer's existing machine. One such component is the unique single-leg rear suspension, which comes complete with hub, brake and wheel as a direct replacement for many existing frames.

The single-leg rear suspension unit. It comes complete with wheel, transmission damper, brake and mudguard.

Nico also supplies his own versions of perfor-mance exhaust systems to fit almost any engine, and not previously mentioned in this account are the beautiful hand-made aluminium petrol tanks, which are fitted to all Bakker machines. Another Bakker-designed component that offers increased performance is the six-piston brake caliper, which can be fitted to most machines and which leads to greater braking efficiency. Finally, to complete any Bakker machine there are electron wheels, tailored seats, and road and race fairings.

With such a complete range of products, and their now-proven performance and quality, Nico Bakker has made his mark on the motorcycle frater-nity, who must be wondering about the next sur-prise to come from the Dutch factory. He has already introduced some firsts for production road bikes: all-aluminium frames, rising-rate rear suspen-sion, universal single-leg rear suspension, the six-piston brake caliper and, to crown all, the QCS.

CHAPTER

2

◼◼◼◼◼◼ Bimota

For many years, Bimota has maintained a reputation for designing and building exciting motorcycles, exciting on three counts: excellent styling, superb finish, and ever-advancing technical design. High-performance machines for both road and track use have been, and continue to be, produced to the now-established superb Bimota quality.

Unlike most independent motorcycle frame makers, Bimota was not formed to manufacture motorcycles. In fact, originally the company had no connection with motorcycles at all. Bimota was founded in 1966 by Valerio Bianchi, Guiseppe Morri and Massimo Tamburrini. The company name was arrived at by combining the first two letters of each founder member's name. The new company was based in Rimini, and was formed to manufacture heating and ventilation ducting. Two of the founders, Guiseppe Morri and Massimo Tamburrini, were motorcycle enthusiasts, which is why Bimota became involved in the motorcycle world.

Massimo Tamburrini soon began to make use of the company's facilities to work on his own beloved motorcycles. Before long, he decided to design and build complete chassis for his bikes. The success of his early work led to more design and construction, and his obvious talent and abilities were to see a

weekend hobby turn into a serious potential business. This potential was eventually exploited to the full when, in 1973, Bimota began to manufacture motorcycles exclusively.

Today, Bimota are world-famous manufacturers of very prestigious and exclusive motorcycles. This reputation has been gained as a result of certain principles that have been followed by the partners from the very beginning. These are to produce comparatively small numbers of motorcycles by hand, using the best possible materials and designs. To maintain their reputation and share of the market, Bimota have strived to lead the field, where possible, with continued innovation, many of their ideas setting the standard for others to follow.

From the very beginning, Bimota have aimed to produce 'no compromise' motorcycles. They are not designed to satisfy the widest possible market group and, therefore, can be tailored for a very specific purpose. Another important principle is that Bimota impose no budget restrictions on either design or manufacture. They have a wonderful saying: they design and build motorcycles for those people who are prepared to sacrifice everything, in order to sacrifice nothing.

The first Bimota principle is that a motorcycle has to be able to meet the riding requirements of the customer, and not vice versa. This is why Bimota motorcycles offer many different adjustments. They put great effort into producing very stiff frames, which is why their frames are as short as practicable; the greater the length, the greater the flex. Materials are also chosen to enhance stiffness.

Another aspect of Bimota quality is that they aim to hold the closest tolerances possible, which is achieved by the use of innovative electronic design systems, coupled with the highest possible standards of workmanship. An advanced CAD-CAM system offers very precise design parameters, which

One of the first machines built by Bimota. This 1973 HB1 utilized a 750 cc four-cylinder Honda engine. The rider is Luigi Anell.

This machine has a frame manufactured completely from steel tubing.

are then transferred directly to digitally-controlled manufacturing machines. The use of this type of machinery enables a wide variety of components to be machined from solid billets. This achieves the lowest possible weight with the highest possible strength.

All this excellence of design and manufacture is supported by Bimota's research and development department, which ensures that the performance and quality of current models is maintained, through experimentation and testing, while advancing development for future models. Even with this excellent research and development department, Bimota claim that one of the most important test areas for their machines is the race track. Here, technical advances prove their worth, while all-important reliability is put to the test.

To enhance their extensive engineering facilities, Bimota have their own in-house fibreglass department. Apart from the production of their own bodywork and fairings, this also carries out development work on the aerodynamics of motorcycles. This serves to improve performance, as well as maintain the Bimota aim of continually producing innovative designs. This work is often carried out in association with other organisations, such as design studios and universities. This attention to body styling has resulted in Bimota gaining a reputation for avant-garde shapes.

With every effort being made to ensure the ultimate possible quality, the materials used in Bimota's designs are also considered to be the very best for each frame. Where steel tubing is used for a space frame or sub-frame, only chromemolybdenum tubing is employed. As a large percentage of chassis are now manufactured in alloys, these materials need very special selection. In Bimota's case, they utilize some of the expensive alloys to be found in the aerospace industries, materials such as Anticorodal, Anticorodal 100 and Avional. These types of alloy enable the best strength-to-weight ratio to be achieved.

It is not sufficient simply to use top-quality materials in the manufacture of motorcycle frames. Of equal importance is the method by which component parts are joined together. To this end, Bimota are keen advocates of thin welding, which looks better, and is structurally better.

For this type of welding, detailed attention must be paid to the parts being welded. The mating faces must fit very accurately prior to welding, as close-fitting components only require a very thin weld to effect a perfect joint. The resultant weld looks better, but more importantly, offers better structural performance.

Thin, even welding is less likely to contain blow-holes and other foreign matter, while those close

tolerances needed at the joints mean that less stress is built into the frame during the welding process, since the weld does not have to pull the mating parts together and close large gaps. To reduce distortion during welding, Bimota have adopted the single-spot-weld method to hold components together initially, after which the weld area is filled in as a secondary operation.

Such attention to detail does assist in the aim for top quality, but is much more time consuming and, therefore, much more expensive.

Having made every effort to produce an accurate, top-quality frame, Bimota spare no effort in protecting it. To this end, the steel frames are electrolytically degreased, then finished with a plastic coating. This has great advantages in that it has a very good appearance, while being more flexible than most paints and lacquers. Therefore, it is more damage resistant.

Aluminium frames and components manufactured by Bimota are anodized to protect their surfaces. The anodized finish becomes part of the surface itself, so is less likely to be porous or crack with any flexing of the frame in use.

There is no production line in the Bimota factory; each machine is assembled by a skilled technician, who is responsible for that machine from start to finish. The technician's name is recorded against the frame number, so that if there are any problems or warranty claims on the machine, the company can trace who built it.

Each motorcycle built by Bimota is tested thoroughly prior to delivery, all the electrics being carefully checked, and the mechanical aspects being given the same detailed inspection. High-quality fibreglass bodywork encapsulates the machine.

As well as excellent materials and manufacture,

Above *The S B 4 with a Suzuki 1100 cc engine. Note the use of machined aluminium alloy to link the frame tubes and form the swinging rear fork pivot.*

Above left *A Kawasaki engine housed in a tubular steel frame with alloy swinging rear fork pivot, which was the standard arrangement for the period.*

Left *The H B 2, again steel tubing with an alloy rear fork pivot. This 1981 model has a 900 cc Honda engine.*

each Bimota features as many technical advantages as possible, allowing the rider to set up his motorcycle to optimize its rideability. To this end, many of the frame's settings are adjustable. Triple clamps allow adjustment of the front end in every possible direction, which means that height, rake and offset can be set to their best advantages, and weight distribution optimized.

One very useful option on many Bimota models is an adjustable steering head angle. This is achieved by means of an eccentric system, coupled with unique conical bearings incorporating specially-shaped rollers. Further adjustment is also made

possible by the use of front forks in which the spring preload can be varied by turning a knob at the top of each leg. In the centre of each knob is a screw, which can be used to set rebound damping.

Like so many independently-produced motorcycles, Bimotas were race-bred from the very beginning. The first official machine was produced in 1973. It was based on a tubular frame and housed a 750 cc, four-cylinder Honda engine. It also had double front disc brakes and carried a top-half fairing. This machine was raced by Luigi Anelli.

For 1974 Bimota utilized Yamaha engines in the Y B 1, 350 cc and 250 cc versions being produced. Then, in 1975, they produced motorcycles with Suzuki engines, the S B 1 being a 500 cc version. Another 500 cc engine used that year was the Aermacchi, this machine being designated A B 1.

Bimota chose a wider range of engines for 1976, frames being designed and built to house Yamaha 350 cc and 250 cc engines (Y B 2), Aermacchi 250 cc engine (A B 2), and Morbidelli 250 cc engines. In the following year, 1977, they designed and built frames for larger-capacity engines, in the form of the S B 2, which housed 750 cc Suzuki

engines, and the KB1, which accepted the Kawasaki engine.

In 1978 Bimota made good use of Yamaha 250 cc and 350 cc engines in the YB3 model, while 1979 was to see the first 1000 cc-engined model. The SB3 utilized a 1000 cc Suzuki engine.

For 1980 500 cc engines from Kawasaki were used in the KB2 models, while in 1981 Bimota designed and built frames for the Honda 900 cc

engine. This model was designated HB2. By 1982 the larger-capacity engines were in demand, and to cater for this Bimota built machines to house the Kawasaki 1100 designated KB3.

Big 1100 cc engines were chosen again for 1983, the SB4 model employing a Suzuki powerplant. That year also saw Bimota take another significant step forward with the introduction of the first Tesi model. This design, designated 2H, was totally

Above *The high-performance Furano, which features race-style bodywork and the usual aluminium alloy twin-spar frame. Upside-down forks take care of the front suspension and steering, while the engine is a 1000 cc Yamaha with integrated ignition and fuel injection.*

Above left *The Bellaria is based on the standard Bimota aluminium alloy twin-spar frame and running gear, clad with stylish, full bodywork. This model is powered by a Yamaha 600 cc engine.*

Left *The Biposto, a two-seat version of the popular Dieci.*

new. It dispensed with conventional front forks. Instead, the front suspension consisted of a swinging-arm arrangement with hub-centre steering. The rear suspension was also based on a swinging arm. Both front and rear swinging arms were damped by a single shock absorber. This development was to become a very important feature of the Bimota range. The first model utilized a 400 cc Honda engine.

In 1984 1100 cc engines were popular, and Bimota marketed two versions: the S B 5, a Suzuki version; and the H B 3, a Honda-engined model. Also that year, Bimota took the exciting Tesi a leap forward with the introduction of a 750 cc version. Again, the engine was a Honda.

Bimota demonstrated their versatility and innovative approach again in 1985, with the use of yet another make of engine. The D B 1 housed a 750 cc Ducati. In 1986 the Yamaha 750 cc engine powered the Y B 4 model, while the Y B 3 utilized the Yamaha 1200. However, the latest version of Tesi, the 3H, was still built around a Honda 750.

A 750 cc Yamaha powered the Y B 4 in 1987, while the Y B 6 had a 1000 cc Yamaha engine. A similar powerplant was fitted to the Y B 4 E X U P in 1988, by which time the popular Tesi model had a 750 cc Yamaha as an option.

In 1989 the Yamaha 1000 cc engine was utilized in the Y B 8 model. That year saw a new model introduced, the Bellaria. This was powered by a 600 cc engine. Another new model was the Tuatara, which had a 1000 cc engine.

Yamaha engines were still in big demand for 1990, and Bimota responded with the Y B 1 0, the 1000 cc version. Tesi, the forkless design, was to see another engine utilized: the model 1D housed an 851 cc Ducati. Bimota also produced a G P 500 cc design during this period.

This account of the main engines used since the company began the production of motorcycles is by no means a full account of Bimota's output, or the range of designs and machines built during that period. From the very beginning, Bimota have been very versatile and innovative, producing both road and racing machines with great success.

The current catalogued range of road bikes, developed as a result of wide experience of what riders want, is impressive and comprehensive. It includes the Dieci, which has an alloy twin-spartype frame, upside-down front forks and monoshock rear suspension. The engine is a four-cylinder, 1000 cc Yamaha. This machine is enclosed by a full set of bodywork that encapsulates the fuel tank and the top portion of the alloy frame. The result is a high-quality, high-performance touring bike in solo form; Biposto, or two-seater, version is also catalogued.

The Y B 8 E uses a twin-spar alloy frame and, again, the 1000 cc Yamaha engine. Race-style bodywork results in a high-performance sports machine. Another version of the Y B 8 E, known as the Furano, has a similar specification, with the exception that it has an integrated ignition and fuel injection system in place of the normal four-carburettor set-up. The use of fuel injection leads to improved engine efficiency and, in turn, significantly improved performance.

The Bellaria uses a similar rolling chassis to the Dieci model, but has its own distinctive full bodywork, and is powered by a Yamaha 600. The result is a stylish touring machine of lower capacity, which was the first two-seater produced by Bimota.

The pride of the fleet is the very exciting Tesi 1D

906R. This is the chassis with swinging-arm front suspension and hub-centre steering. Aluminium alloy is used for the frame, while full stylish bodywork totally encapsulates the machine. This exciting package is powered by a 904 cc, twin-cylinder, liquid-cooled Ducati engine, which has an integrated ignition and fuel injection system, and desmodromic valve gear.

There is also a Tesi 1D E S, which is a special-edition model with distinctive bodywork. This was produced to celebrate 20 years of Bimota.

The 904 cc Ducati engine is also utilized in the DB 2, which is offered in full- and half-fairing versions. It is a lightweight performance model with excellent handling characteristics.

Most of the Bimota range described here have aluminium alloy frames, although the DB 2 frame is manufactured from high-quality steel tubing. The complete machine weighs in at an amazingly low 164 kg (362 lb) for the half-fairing version, and 168 kg (370 lb) for the full-fairing model. By comparison, apart from the Bellaria at 175 kg (386 lb) all the other Bimota models weigh at least 180 kg (397 lb) or more.

As this account shows, Bimota have been very progressive since they began in 1973, making advances in technical aspects and in quality, as well as being aware of their customers' requirements. All this has resulted in considerable growth and produced a well established company that has the respect of the motorcycling fraternity throughout the world.

Gucci, Ferrari – Bimota

Bimota have established themselves as a large, independent manufacturer of advanced motorcycle designs, built to the highest possible standards. Although they have become prolific builders of road and sport machines, since the company was formed, they have also designed and built many excellent racing machines. These have proved very competitive, to the extent of winning 350 races world-wide. Bimota's own factory team has lifted three world championships and over 20 Italian championships, a competition record that any manufacturer would be very proud of. The list of famous riders to race Bimota machines is also impressive and includes the great Agostini, Read,

Lucchinelli, Cecotto, Vucini, Villa, Ekerold, Pileri, Ferrari, Lavado, Mertens and Falappa.

This account illustrates the capability and potential of Bimota. It is impossible to guess what innovation the company will come up with next, but one wonder's how long it will be before they produce their own engine. If such an engine was of the same quality and performance as their current products, the wait would be worthwhile.

Below The half-fairing version of the exciting D B 2. The frame is high-quality steel tubing, and the engine a Ducati of 904 cc. With a total dry weight of 164 kg (362 lb), the machine has an excellent power-to-weight ratio.

The later Tesi 1D. Powered by a 904 cc twin-cylinder Ducati engine, this stylish machine is an excellent example of Bimota's capabilities.

The prototype of Bimota's advanced-technology Tesi. In place of conventional front forks is a swinging arm with hub-centre steering. This model is powered by a 400 cc Honda engine.

CHAPTER

3

▮▮▮▮▮▮ Dresda Autos

Dave Degens received an excellent training in engineering in his father's business during the 1950s, obtaining a wide variety of skills. This background was to prove invaluable later. He developed a passion for motorcycles at an early age, and his new-found engineering skills were soon utilized to carry out modifications, improvements and repairs to a number of machines.

Dave's skills led to contact with Dresda Autos, a retail scooter outlet that took some machines modified by him on a sale-or-return basis. When the owners of Dresda Autos became disenchanted with the shop in 1963, Dave Degens stepped in and bought it. He retained their best scooter mechanic and carried on the retail business, but also added motorcycles to the range.

Although it retained the name, it was inevitable that Dresda's business would change. For as well as being a very competitive racing motorcyclist, Dave Degens had built three Tritons (a marriage of a Triumph engine and a Norton featherbed frame) and a Norton Rocket prior to buying the shop. There was a ready demand for these high-performance motorcycles and, as a result, Dresda Autos was to become the prolific builder of high-quality, high-performance motorcycles we know today.

Having built motorcycles for his own and other people's use long before he started the business, Dave Degens was clearly very capable, even at this early stage. A very valuable addition to his engineering skill was his riding skill; at this point, his racing experience was considerable.

Dave Degens had gained his racing experience by successfully competing on such machines as BSA Gold Stars, AJS, 7Rs, and of course, Tritons. His racing experience was not always on the larger, powerful-engined machines, however, and he is rather proud of a very successful outing on a twin-cylinder Rumi scooter in a race catering for that type of machine.

After buying Dresda Autos, he continued to race motorcycles; in fact, his riding had not gone unnoticed by others. During the 1964 season, one of the

works BMW riders was unable to ride in the 24-hour endurance race in Barcelona, Spain, and Dave was offered the ride. This was his introduction to endurance racing, and it was during this race that he proved to have a flair for night riding. As a result, he did much of the night stint.

The experience of riding the BMW fired his enthusiasm for endurance racing, and he was soon making plans to build a bike and compete in his own right. This was no dream. He engineered a Triumph engine into a Manx Norton featherbed frame, and another Triton was born. With this machine he went to Barcelona for the 1965 24-hour race and won it.

Having won the Spanish race, in his usual quest to progress, he decided to put a 650 cc Triumph engine into a specially-made lightweight Dresda frame for the same event. With this machine, he

Left Dave Degens working on the construction of a Triton in the early days of Dresda Autos, in 1965.

Above This machine was a combination of a Dresda frame and a Honda engine. It gave the company one of its early major victories by winning the 24-hour Bol d'Or endurance race.

Right An early Dresda frame just after the welding has been completed. This particular frame was made to house a Triumph twin.

won again in 1970. He is the only Englishman to have won the Barcelona 24-hour race on an English bike, a feat that he accomplished twice.

Dave Degens' ability to produce the best of the superb Triton hybrids was now well and truly proven, leading to an excellent and exciting line of business. However, although the Triton offered Dresda Autos a positive line of business, it didn't prevent him from exercising his skills on other interesting projects. One such opportunity arose during 1968, when he solved a problem for Yamaha, who were experiencing difficulties with the swinging rear fork of their racing machines. The problem was a pivot bearing fault, which Dave first identified and then cured by modifying the assembly.

This was not the last of the Yamaha swinging rear fork modifications carried out by Dave, although the next project was more of a manufacturing task than one of modification. He was engaged to build a new rear fork to accommodate a racing tyre that had come onto the market. The new tyre was too large for the factory-supplied fork, so Dave made a new fork from box-section steel. Some of those who rode the Degens modified machines include Christian Sarron, Rodney Gould and the legendary Barry Sheene.

In 1969 Dresda Autos produced a chassis to house the Triumph 500 cc Daytona engine. The new frame was built from 17 swg Reynolds 531 tubing, and when completed it weighed-in at only 64 kg (141 lb). This lightweight machine made its racing début at Snetterton, ridden by the designer and builder himself, Dave Degens. It finished in an exciting second place, by no more than a wheel, after a race-long battle with the works Triumph,

Opposite, above *Another early Dresda machine, utilizing a Suzuki 500.*

Opposite, below *A typical frame kit, in this case for a four-cylinder Honda engine.*

Left *A model from the early 1980s, the engine being a 750 cc K-series Honda.*

Below *This machine demonstrates the versatility of Dresda Autos, the frame accommodating a Honda Gold Wing engine. It was built in 1983 for Ken Hull of Honda UK.*

ridden by the famous Percy Tate. Two weeks later, Degen used it to win the Scarborough Gold Cup. Both this and the Snetterton event were full International meetings, proving that both machine and rider were up to scratch.

During the 1970–1 period, Dresda Autos won a contract to produce a batch of five frames for Christian Vilaseca. These were designed and built by Dresda to house Honda 750 cc engines. The plan was for Dresda to build the complete frames, then Christian Vilaseca would fit the engines: but soon after delivery an urgent call to Dave Degens suggested that the engines would not fit the frames.

Having built the frames, Degens knew that all was correct, but could not convince the customer of this, so a friendly wager was set. The deal was that

Above *This 1977 race bike was built to compete in Spanish national events, the colour scheme being that of the Spanish bank that sponsored the rider. The engine is a 750 cc K-series Honda.*

Above left *A short-stroke 350 cc Triumph engine in a Dresda race frame.*

Left *A 750 cc Honda-engined drag bike built by Dresda Autos for Terry Revel. It was a record holder in its class.*

Right *A one-off frame for a four-cylinder Kawasaki.*

Below right *A typical Dresda Triton, comprising a Norton frame and an electric-start Triumph engine. Note the low seat position. This example was built to order for a customer in Japan.*

he would fly to Paris to fit, or attempt to fit, an engine. If the engine did go into the frame, Vilaseca would cover the cost of the trip; if it didn't, Dresda would pay for the visit and rectify the faulty frames.

On arrival at the Paris factory, Dave soon spotted why they could not fit the engine. The mechanics were trying to lift it into the frame, but the space between the frame tubes didn't appear large enough. He promptly laid the engine on the workshop floor and then fed the frame over it, passing it over the narrowest part of the engine, then moving it to the correct mounting position.

After the drama, these Dresda-supplied frames fared well. One of the Christian Vilaseca machines went on to win the prestigious Bol d'Or 24-hour race, while two more finished in the top six.

The success achieved by Dresda and their products gained the company a high reputation, which resulted in an approach by Yamaha who wanted a frame to house one of their 750 cc twin-cylinder engines. Dresda were supplied a complete bike, from which the engine was removed and fitted into the Dresda frame. It was during this project that Dave Degens' forward thinking showed itself once more, when he incorporated monoshock rear suspension, quite an advance for the early 1970s.

The Yamaha project was to show that Dave Degens' skills also extend to engines, as the particular type of Yamaha 750 cc engine suffered a persistent internal problem. He not only established the cause of the problem, but also carried out modifications to eliminate it. This work led to a contract for Dresda to follow the fault right through, including visiting the Porsche test centre where development on the engine was being carried out. Dave Degens oversaw the various modifications, and also developed a further mod to rectify a fault that caused the cam chain to destroy its tensioner.

While at the test centre, Dave became aware that an engine under test was not running correctly. He discovered that the throttle slides were fitted incorrectly. Much to everyone's amazement, he corrected the throttle set-up, and the engine achieved the power output expected.

With a successful development frame for Yamaha and the engine work, Dave Degens and Dresda

Autos had shown their potential to this important manufacturer and the motorcycling public. From the very beginning, they had also shown motorcycling enthusiasts that almost any engine could benefit from a Dresda frame. The range of engines fitted to Dresda frames is quite extensive and speaks volumes for their versatility. It includes Triumph, Norton, B S A, Suzuki, Honda, and Kawasaki.

Top The type of machine for which Dresda are renowned: a Triumph triple in a Norton frame.

Above Dave Degens in action during 1990. The machine, of course, is a Dresda Triumph.

Right Man and machine: Dave Degens with his personal Dresda Triumph during 1991. Both see a full season on the track.

In addition to their impressive frames, Dresda Autos also market their own swinging rear fork kit, and have from the beginning offered a comprehensive modification service. They will modify the frame to take an alternative engine, or convert a dual shock absorber system to monoshock suspension, and carry out special frame modifications, such as adding extra tubes to enhance stiffness.

In fact, Dave Degens' skills have been called upon for an endless, indefinable list of one-off modifications. His unrivalled range of experience makes him and Dresda Autos ideally suited to the needs of the specialist motorcycle enthusiast.

Design and ride

Any business that operated from 1963 to the present and was still very active would be considered in anyone's terms long-running. But given the very competitive environment in which Dresda Autos operates, this is a considerable achievement. This enviable position is attributable to its proprietor, Dave Degens.

Although Dave will have had excellent skilled hands working for him over the years, his own proven skills, coupled with his forward thinking and many other abilities, are without doubt the basis of Dresda's success. As this account shows, he and Dresda Autos have been involved in many differing motorcycle projects over the years, most with great success. One point stands out from all this, however: that Dave Degens began by building a Triton, and after all these years the Dresda Triton is still the company's main line of business.

Dave Degens has one ability that has always been valuable to his line of business and that has given him great personal pleasure: his riding ability. When the designer can take his latest creation onto the circuit and ride it to its potential, this has to be a great advantage. Most other manufacturers have to rely on feedback from a professional rider, which is open to misinterpretation.

For many years, Dresda Autos have produced beautifully-engineered motorcycles, greatly treasured by enthusiasts. If Dave Degens has his way, they will continue to do so.

4

▮▮▮▮▮▮ *Egli Motorradtechnik AG*

In the field of motorcycle frame design and manufacture, the name Fritz Egli is legendary. Over many years, his reputation for innovation, performance, finish and excellent engineering has become widespread.

Like many other frame makers, Fritz Egli became involved initially by carrying out modifications to improve the performance of existing equipment. With this type of natural talent and flair, it was inevitable that he would move on to greater things. The motorcycling world now knows the level of his achievement and potential.

Fritz Egli raced motorcycles himself, which gave him first-hand knowledge of what was required from a particular frame. This direct experience proved invaluable in the short and long term. The short term aspect was that, prior to forming his business, Fritz raced a Vincent. Its many handling problems, which on occasion produced alarming speed wobbles, resulted in a difficult machine to ride. Concerted effort and courage in his riding produced just a single third place over a considerable period.

At this point, Egli made a far-reaching decision: to design and build a new frame for the Vincent. This new frame had a major influence on the fortunes of its designer and builder.

The immediate effect of the new frame was very evident, for Fritz Egli won every race he entered in 1968, taking the Swiss Championship. This remarkable improvement in the performance of the Vincent proved two major points: firstly, that the right frame is vital to the ultimate performance of the motorcycle; secondly, that Fritz Egli could both design and build successful motorcycle frames. The die was cast, and many future customers would reap the benefit of his obvious engineering talents.

Egli had actually begun using his engineering talent as a business during 1965. Since then, he has gone from strength to strength, and his reputation

Above *For road or track, the Red Hunter makes use of a four-cylinder Honda engine of up to 1200 cc.*

Below left *The Egli Red Falcon, which can accommodate Honda or Yamaha single-cylinder engines from 500 to 650 cc.*

for versatility and quality is well known throughout the motorcycling world.

'Versatility' is almost an understatement. Since the business began, the list of frames produced for differing engines is almost endless. Moreover, those frames have been built for many different uses. In addition to the beautiful road bikes for which Fritz Egli has become famous, he has also produced many competition frames, the majority for road racing, for which he has a special enthusiasm and, of course, first-hand knowledge.

The successful Vincent frame was followed during this early period by frames to house such engines as the famous Triumph twin, and later the triple. This was a very active period, as these engines had become very popular. Egli went on to build frames for Honda 450 cc twins and the larger, very popular 750 cc four-cylinder version, together with a range of Kawasaki engines, including the H2 and H3. Yamaha two-stroke engines were well utilized too, most of these for road racing machines with capacities of 250 cc, 350 cc and 750 cc.

Laverda, Ducati and Suzuki engines have all been given the Egli treatment; even the ever-popular American Harley-Davidson engine has found its way into a Fritz Egli frame. Another famous make to benefit from Egli's skills was the German BMW.

The utilization of such a wide range of engines illustrates the versatility of Fritz Egli's engineering skills. These are all the more impressive when you consider that the range of engines listed covers many different cubic capacities, physical sizes and layouts, and that the frames were built for differing purposes.

Egli machines have been built for road racing, where handling is a critical factor, and his road-going machines are world renowned. However, Egli frames have also been seen in drag racing form, and he has produced sidecar outfits for such engines as Suzuki and the Yamaha V MAX.

In over 20 years of frame production, two significant points stand out in all the Egli designs. One is the persistent use of the rigid backbone layout; almost all Egli frames use a version of this arrangement. The other point is that Fritz Egli has never waivered from the use of steel tubing in the manufacture of his frames.

The performance and popularity of Fritz Egli machines, the latter illustrated by the large numbers produced, prove that his designs and quality of

For four-cylinder Kawasaki engines, Egli customers can choose the Bonneville.

manufacture have been of technological excellence from the beginning. Every frame is completely nickel-plated, adding to the reputation for superlative finish that all Egli machines possess.

Although Fritz Egli has built many one-off machines for a wide variety of engines, he is one of the few independent frame manufacturers to catalogue a range of standard designs. This covers widely differing specifications to meet the requirements of the motorcycling world.

This book is about frame makers, but no account of this type would be complete without mention of Fritz Egli's engine tuning abilities. This talent encompasses the major tuning skills: gas flowing cylinder heads; special cams; re-worked crankshafts, valve gear and pistons; and tailored exhaust systems. With these skills at hand, the excellent reputation and performance achievements of Fritz Egli come as no surprise.

The standard production Egli machines cover most needs of high-performance race and road-going motorcycles. They have included the Red Lightning II, reported at the time (1990) to be one of the fastest street-legal production motorcycles in the world.

Red Lightning utilized a typical backbone frame with front forks of Egli design. This set-up housed a Suzuki GSX engine bored out to 1258 cc and fitted with 11:1 Cosworth pistons, driving a lightened and reworked standard Suzuki crank. Enlarged Cosworth valves were operated by Megacycle cams, while extensive gas flowing of the head was enhanced by Egli's own free-flow exhaust system. The powerplant was fed by a 36 mm Mikuni carburettor.

The engine produced 170 fps at the gearbox at 9200 rpm. Maximum torque of 14·8 kgm was achieved at 7300 rpm. One unusual item offered by Fritz Egli is an autographic record of this performance data for each engine sold.

Although the standard Suzuki five-speed gearbox was utilized, internal modifications were carried out to make it capable of handling the extra power. The standard clutch was replaced by an American Barnett unit, which proved itself capable of coping with the extra power very well.

One test showed the Egli RL2 to have a top speed of 441 kph (274 mph). The fact that larger-capacity versions were available made this a machine for experienced pilots.

At the time of writing, the catalogued models offer both performance and style, and meet all the current trends. They include the Egli Turbo, a refined replica of the legendary MRD1. This utilizes the Kawasaki four-cylinder engine in 1100–1200 cc capacities, and is fully turbocharged. It weighs in at 212 kg (467 lb), and with 180–250 bhp available – depending on boost pressure – makes for a bike with phenomenal performance potential. Acceleration from 0–200 kph (0–124 mph) is achieved in just 7·2 seconds. The world record machine (same engine, but higher boost and larger coolers) showed 290bhp on the dyno. This bike clocked 320 kph (202·5 mph) at Nardo, Southern Italy, with a top-half fairing only.

To achieve such outstanding performance, the engine internals received considerable attention from Egli, and many specialized engine components were fitted. These included a special Egli oil pump that delivered 30 per cent more oil than the standard pump, and an alcohol-water injection system. If required, N_2O injection could be fitted, resulting in 50 per cent more power. Specially forged pistons ran in Nikasil-coated aluminium cylinder liners, topped by modified cylinder heads. A perfectly balanced crankshaft handled the power, which was transmitted to the rear wheel through a reinforced clutch.

One important aspect of this remarkable powerplant was a special racing turbo ignition system that was automatically retarded in proportion to turbocharger boost pressure. As with most Egli performance engines, custom-built exhaust headers enhanced the efficiency of the whole set-up.

One of Fritz Egli's superb cantilever frames housed that remarkable powerplant. Egli front forks took care of the steering, while a gas shock absorber controlled the rear suspension. The result was a machine with the stability necessary to cope with the immense power.

The MRD1 Replica is a machine that is only recommended for riders with considerable experience of this level of performance. This point is taken one stage further by the fact that although this machine could be supplied as a two-seater, Egli does not recommend it.

Another standard high-performance machine is the Bonneville. Again, this uses a four-cylinder Kawasaki engine, in capacities of 750–1200 cc. The frame is a nickel-plated backbone type, with cantilever swinging rear fork controlled by a gas shock absorber. The machine has exactly the same frame layout as that which Jacques Cornu used to beat the works machines and set a new lap record in the long-distance world championship for Formula 1, held at the Nürburgring in 1981. This machine is as much at home on the race track as it is delivering high performance on the street.

Although the Bonneville is a catalogued design, there is a long list of optional equipment that can be used to tailor the machine to the customer's requirements in terms of performance and aesthetics. This equipment includes wheels of different sizes and rim widths, race-bred brake components, selected instruments, alternative gear ratios, and much more. The entire package can be enclosed in an aerodynamically-perfected fairing.

Also in Egli's catalogues is the Red Hunter. This uses a similar frame to the Bonneville, but is designed to accept Honda four-cylinder in-line engines of 750–1200 cc. The usual range of engine options is available so that the Honda user can take advantage of the renowned Egli engine tuning service. In conjunction with Shüle, the German exhaust specialist, Egli has developed a 4-2-1 exhaust system for the Honda four-cylinder engines. This produces an 8–10 bhp increase in the medium rpm range, with a weight saving of 7·2 kg (16 lb). The Red Hunter is another of Fritz Egli's powerful machines that handle well, and are at

home on the race track and the road. It is recommended for use by riders with considerable experience.

Due to the renewed interest of a large number of the world's motorcyclists in single-cylinder engines, Fritz Egli produces an ultra-light sports machine that caters for the single-cylinder enthusiast, the Red Falcon. The interesting point about this machine is that two standard versions are catalogued: one for a Honda engine, the other for a Yamaha. However, it can be made to order with other single-cylinder engines.

Similar frames are used for both versions of the Red Falcon. Again, the nickel-plated, rigid backbone type is utilized. Standard engine capacities are 500–600 cc.

The components that make up the Bonneville kit.

The Honda engine offered is of the wet-sump type, oil being contained in the crankcase. The Yamaha version features dry-sump lubrication, an oil tank being built into the frame. As with all Fritz Egli motorcycles, the Red Falcon is offered with a wide range of chassis component options, while the engines can be supplied in any state of tune required, there being the usual range of special engine parts to enhance performance.

Apart from complete machines, Fritz Egli also catalogues a very wide range of special parts for both chassis and engines. From the chassis point of view, these include special wheels, brake components and systems, forks and suspension parts, and much more. Engine parts include high-performance pistons, crankshafts, oil pumps and cams. All have been developed over the years to be utilized by Egli himself on customers' machines, or even for customers to carry out their own tuning work. And, of course, to finish the machine, there is a range of fairing options.

For a manufacturer famous for such a wide range of high-performance motorcycles, Fritz Egli's latest business project comes as a bit of a surprise. He is importing Indian-built Enfields – a reminder of the once-glorious British motorcycle industry, now in exile but thriving.

The Madras-based factory has produced the Enfield range for a considerable number of years, and when Fritz discovered this he bought four and ran them for a year to see how they performed. He was prompted to do this out of nostalgia, as the first motorcycle he owned had been a 350 cc Royal Enfield Bullet. Although the Indian-built Enfields had become popular, their quality of construction

had been criticised. However, Fritz felt that some of the problems could be eradicated and further improvements made. These improvements are centred on blueprinting, that is improving the engineering quality in some areas of the machine, while in some cases engine modifications are made to improve performance.

In 1992 Fritz became an importer of the Indian bikes, and developed his own pre-delivery improvement programme for each machine sold. The frame is checked for straightness, and corrected if necessary, while the wheels and spokes are checked and trued-up where needed. The forks are stripped completely, all the components being deburred and polished. New dual-rate springs are fitted, together with special low-friction oil seals. The front brake is overhauled and machined where necessary for roundness. Various options are available, such as different handlebars, alloy wheel rims and Koni adjustable rear shock absorbers.

The cylinder head and barrel are stripped, and the head flange machined to closely match the barrel, thus dispensing with the normal head gasket. This improves heat transfer and raises the compression slightly to 7:1. Valve seats are machined to line up accurately with the valve guides, and blended into the combustion chamber and ports. The valve spring seats are modified to give the correct height, while the rocker gear is ground to achieve correct alignment and to reduce some weight. The ignition system is reworked, a new carburettor manifold installed, and the carburettor itself fitted with a different slide and needle. An Egli high-output oil pump replaces the original. Other changes include a new kickstart and gear lever.

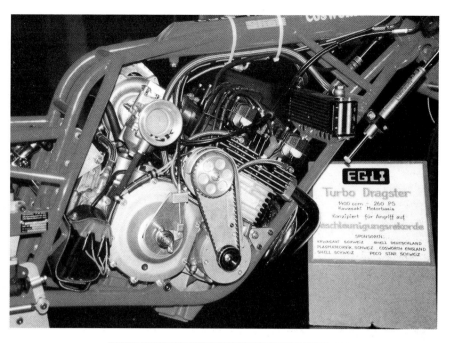

Left *The famous Suzuki Red Lightning II. With its Egli-reworked engine, it was one of the fastest road-going production machines available.*

Right *This one-off is a turbocharged Kawasaki-engined machine built for drag racing.*

Below right *Egli's latest project is as an importer, and improver, of the classic-style Enfields from India. This example is the Bullet Classic Solo.*

The gearbox is stripped, all parts being deburred and polished. A new bronze layshaft is bushed and fitted, while the gear selectors are engineered to achieve a smooth, reliable action. Gearing is altered to suit the particular model; other changes include a new kickstart and gear lever. The clutch is also stripped, and the drum lining faces machined flat, the steel discs being slotted. Then everything is carefully reassembled.

Apart from producing an enjoyable and reliable machine, the Egli treatment also improves performance. For example, a standard Indian-built 500 cc Bullet develops 22 bhp, while the Egli version delivers 26 bhp.

In addition to the improved stock 500 cc Bullet, Fritz also offers two larger-capacity versions. One has a capacity of 535 cc, being bored out from 84 to 87 mm and utilizing a special piston. Large valves improve breathing, while an alloy cylinder barrel (which is 3 kg/7 lb lighter) replaces the standard cast-iron cylinder. This 535 version of the Bullet produces 45 bhp at 5100 rpm.

To top the lot, however, Fritz offers the 624 cc Super Bullet. This version has the same mods as the 535, with the addition of a long-stroke crankshaft. It also runs a higher compression ratio at 8·9:1; the stock compression is 6·5:1. This Super Bullet produces an exciting 47 bhp at 5100 rpm, with more torque throughout the rev range.

For those seeking the looks and ride of the classic era, these Indian-built, Egli-improved Enfields are bound to have an appeal. This is borne out by the fact that Fritz sold 52 in the very first year, while 90 machines were projected for the following year. The machine not only gives the bike world another

interesting product, but it also adds another string to Fritz Egli's powerful and accurate bow.

Backbone of steel

Over the 20 years or so that Fritz Egli has been applying his considerable engineering talents to the production of motorcycles for race and road use, his reputation for both performance and finish has become legendary. Not only has he produced a wide range of machines for many uses, but he has also manufactured very large numbers of some types. One would only have to attend an Egli owners' meeting to appreciate how popular and sought-after are the motorcycles from this long-established, independent frame maker.

The demand for Fritz Egli motorcycles is still strong world-wide, so these beautiful high-performance machines will continue to be produced for many years to come. Moreover, with Fritz Egli's continued enthusiasm, and his quest for performance and perfection from whatever engines become available, that demand is sure to continue.

CHAPTER

5

IIIIIII **Harris Performance Products**

As an independent motorcycle frame manufacturer Harris Performance Products needs no introduction; their fame is world-wide. For many years, they have built a wide variety of successful machines for many renowned riders. The business was formed in 1972 by two brothers, Steve and Lester Harris. Engineering apprenticeships gave both the right background.

Steve and Lester worked for different companies, but both worked on the manufacture of race cars, Lester also being involved in the construction of go-karts. As the cars and karts of that period were tubular framed, the Harris brothers gained great experience in this form of construction, which was to prove invaluable later.

Although encouraged to race cars, the brothers turned to their first love, motorcycles. Both enjoyed successful club racing careers, which began on BSA A65s. Over the next few years, they found success on a variety of machines, including a Seeley G50, 7 R A G S Triumph Bonnevilles and, towards their latter days of racing, T R 500 Suzukis.

As enthusiastic clubman racers with engineering backgrounds, the brothers carried out many modifications to their machines over the years to improve performance. The extent of these modifications grew continuously until eventually they began to build complete frames. Their work did not go unnoticed, and it led to an increasing number of requests for similar modifications and frames from those less able to carry out this type of work for themselves.

With full-time jobs, the brothers had difficulty in finding the time to meet all the requests from other riders, never mind the requirements of their own racing programme. As a result, they decided to utilize their obvious talent on a commercial basis. This led to the formation of Harris Performance Products.

The Harris brothers continued to race for a further year. This and their past racing experience, coupled with their engineering backgrounds, served them well in getting the company off to a good

start. They began by manufacturing a variety of components to meet individual requirements. Exhaust systems were in constant demand. However, any components that differed from the factory chassis or parts could be considered, and the Harris brothers soon achieved a good reputation. This work became steady business, and demand continued to grow.

During the first year, the company produced the first complete frame. This machine incorporated a feature that was considered advanced at the time: a single rear shock absorber, which replaced the widely-used twin shock absorber system where a unit is mounted directly to each leg of the swinging rear fork. Both chassis and swinging rear fork, like all machines at the time, were built from steel tubing. This first complete Harris chassis housed a Suzuki Super 6 engine, which had a capacity of 250 cc.

Lester Harris raced the Suzuki-powered machine for a season, but the engine's very narrow power band made it difficult to race. Despite the engine

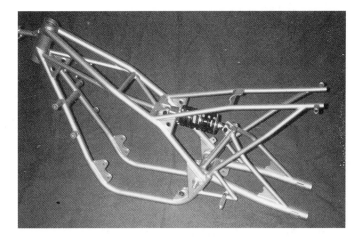

proving unsuitable, the chassis gave good handling. In fact, others saw its worth, and orders for similar frames began to flow into Harris Performance Products from other riders. The Harris brothers were now established as builders of complete bikes.

This very first design was an instant success, and somewhere in the region of 15 were built. All were tailored to accommodate each customer's choice of engine, and these varied considerably. They included Triumph, Yamaha, Crescent and König. An interesting point is that both the Crescent and the König were developed from outboard boat engines, the Crescent being a three-cylinder design.

The ability to design and build their own complete bike set the seal of approval on their ability, and Harris were seen as the people to whom serious racers turned. This was illustrated by the number of their conversions of the very popular over-the-counter Yamaha T Z Racer, from the standard twin shock absorber system to the state-of-the-art single shock absorber.

When the Harrises had been in full-time business for about two years, Steve Bayford joined the firm to handle the import and export of the very latest designs in cycle parts. After establishing and running this successfully for two years, he joined the Harris set-up as a full partner.

Left Harris are justly famous for the quality of their formed aluminium twin spar chassis.

Above This Triton replica frame was built in 1970 to house a Triumph twin engine, before the official formation of Harris Performance Products.

Top In 1972, just after the company came into being, this complete chassis was made to house a Yamaha engine. Although it is of normal layout, note the early use of single shock absorbers.

During the mid 1970s, the Yamaha T Z 700 filled many entries in Formula 750 racing, but was considered by many not to handle too well in the ex-factory state. Consequently, many riders called on Harris Performance Products to supply their own design of rear suspension for this machine. This utilized the now-proven single shock absorber system. Among those who took up this option for the 1976 season were Cork Ballington, Steve

Parish, John Newbold and Mick Grant. To illustrate the impact that the Harris rear end was having at the beginning of the European 750 Formula Championship, of the 32 starters on the grid for the first race at Silverstone, 18 used the Harris rear fork and monoshock.

In 1976–7, the world-renowned Barry Sheene won the world championship for Yamaha. During 1978, the AKAI Yamaha that he was to ride was modified by Harris in an effort to improve its handling. The modifications led to Harris building a complete chassis to house the Yamaha engine during the same season.

Back-to-back tests by Barry demonstrated that the Harris machine was better than the factory example, and he indicated that he wanted to use the machine. Yamaha offered him a full works machine, which had a new alloy chassis, but Barry Sheene insisted on the works engine being fitted to the Harris chassis, and he got his way. This was a very flattering situation for Harris and it proved to the world the esteem in which he was held.

Barry Sheene began the following season on a brand-new full works Yamaha for Grand Prix events. This machine utilized Yamaha's latest alloy chassis. However, he continued to race a Harris chassis in the 750 cc Superbike Championship events, these being the international follow-on from what was the 750 cc European Championship.

During that same season, Barry Sheene was involved in the horrific accident that resulted in both his legs being very badly smashed. The accident happened while he was practising for the British Grand Prix.

Above *The completed T Z 250 Yamaha-engined racer of 1972. The rider was a Harris employee.*

Right *A steel-tubing chassis built in 1974 to house the Suzuki T R 750 engine. Note the concentric rear fork.*

Below right *Mike Trimby on 1975 Harris endurance racer.*

He ran at full speed into the bike of another rider who had fallen after taking a fast corner. So severe were Barry Sheene's injuries that the whole motorcycling world thought that his career was at an end. He was so determined to carry on racing that within a few short weeks he signed a contract to ride for Suzuki. For a short spell he rode Randy Mamola's old machine, but Harris were contracted to build him a chassis, and they continued to build him frames until he retired. This work resulted in the production of the Mk 10.

Although some exciting rides were to come from the Harris/Suzuki/Sheene combination, the best performance from the combination was third place in the South African Grand Prix of 1984. This and several other rides were very creditable, bearing in mind that by then, the Suzuki engine design was becoming very dated.

While supplying Barry Sheene with Grand Prix chassis, Harris Performance were also becoming active in Formula 1. They produced a chassis to house the Kawasaki Z1 900 cc engine, which Andy Goldsmith and Mike Trimby raced successfully in endurance races. The success led to over 400 examples being produced for Formula 1. Between 1980 and 1985, many famous names were to ride Harris

Formula 1 machines. These include Phil Read, Mick Grant, Steve Parish, Trevor Nation and John Newbold. During the early 1980s, Harris also found time to produce motocross chassis to house 250 cc Suzuki engines for use in the world championship by Suzuki UK.

The chassis built for Andy Goldsmith and Mike Trimby had a far-reaching effect on Harris Performance Products. It was their first excursion into the use of a four-cylinder engine, and the performance was impressive enough for Harris to develop a version for Martin Lunde. This he raced with considerable success during 1978–9. The machine was known as the Magnum, and it led to Harris

Performance Products taking a very significant step forward.

Although competing against factory machines, the Magnum proved a serious contender, and resulted in a steady demand for racing versions. However, the obvious potential of this design as a high-performance, up-market, road bike was not overlooked by Harris, and a steady market also developed for the road version.

The name Magnum is now firmly established, but the complete bike – in both race and road trim – has been developed over the years to keep up with requirements of track and road. From concept to the time of writing this book, Harris have produced

Left *The Magnum Mk I.*

Above *Another Magnum Mk I built to a customer's specification.*

form, something that is unique for this class of machine. Harris offer a comprehensive service to the home builder by undertaking any of the assembly work that the customer cannot do. No matter how the Magnum is purchased, it can be tailored to personal requirements.

The customer's donor bike supplies many of the major standard components that fit directly into the Magnum chassis. Any parts of the donor bike that are not suitable are replaced by those from the kit. Although the original Magnum was designed around a Kawasaki, there have been Yamaha, Suzuki- and Honda-based versions. Again, this shows the versatility of the well-proven design.

During 1984–5, Suzuki UK contracted Harris to build machines that, in essence, were replicas of those built previously for Barry Sheene. These had tubular steel chassis.

Suzuki ran a two-bike team using these machines, the riders being Phil Mellor and Mark Phillips, but they also sold to many private owners. These privateers included Trevor Nation, Darren Dixon and Steve Manley. This Harris design proved a lasting favourite with private owners. Riding one of these

over 1000 versions of this marvellous machine.

Magnum has something that makes it very special in both road and track form, and that is versatility. Its well-proven design, based on a fully-triangulated chassis made from Reynolds 531 steel tubing and manganese-bronze welded, forms the basis for a machine that can be supplied fully finished or in kit machines, Mark Phillips won the 1987 British Championship, while in 1988 Darren Dixon won the British Championship. So popular was this design that examples were still being raced in 1990.

During the 1984–5 period, Harris had made considerable advances in the development of aluminium chassis. This led to the production of a version to accept a 250 cc Rotax engine. The chassis incorporated two rectangular box-section alloy extrusions that formed the main part of a twin-spar layout. Strength and stiffness was enhanced in critical areas by the addition of alloy sheet to form further box sections. An alloy rear swinging fork of Harris' design completed the rolling chassis.

The new design, built as a serious 250 cc racer, was supplied to a company called Decorite, who commissioned Harris for the package. This company raced successfully in the 250 cc class, but also very effectively marketed the machine under their own name, resulting in approximately 50 machines being built, a significant number for a pure race machine.

By then, the alloy chassis was becoming state-of-the-art, and Harris continued to develop the use of the material. Other customers, wishing to take advantage of the latest developments and weight-saving qualities, were keen to commission Harris to produce machines to the latest technical levels. One such customer was the well-known Dr J. Urlich.

To begin with, the chassis built for Dr Urlich utilized rectangular, box-section extrusions. Again, the chassis was of the backbone type, with additional boxing where required. This chassis was completed with an alloy swinging rear fork and became the 1985 Mk1. It housed a Rotax 250 cc engine. Using the Harris machine, Dr Urlich successfully raced a full team under the well-known designation of EMC. Harris continued to build for him, producing approximately 12 Mk1 versions, all with alloy extrusions forming the chassis backbone.

In their quest for improvement, Harris had begun to develop the technique of forming alloy sheet to the required box-sections and welding them together. This enabled the chassis to be formed to the required shape and layout without the limitations imposed by standard extrusions. It also allowed the shape to be utilized to enhance the structural performance where required. While this method of chassis manufacture gave more technical scope, it

Top This early 1980s photograph shows Lester Harris handing over a Harris-built machine to its new owner. The engine is a 500 cc Honda.

Above Jim Wells riding one of two Harris entries in the 1984 Formula I TT.

Left *During 1983, Harris designed and built this Formula 1 chassis to house a 1000 cc Kawasaki engine.*

Top left *Rear fork detail of the F1 racer.*

Below left *The frame arrangement of the 1983 Harris-built F1 machine.*

Above *Steve Harris holds the frame for another F1 machine, built in late 1984 for a GPZ 750 Kawasaki.*

Above right *The complete Kawasaki-based F1 machine.*

Right *During 1984–5, Harris designed and built an alloy chassis to house a Rotax 250. The work was carried out for a company called Decorite, who were to race the machine. Success on the track led to approximately 50 of these machines being sold. Note the use of extrusions and formed alloy components.*

Top *The Decorite 250 in action.*

Above *A steel-tubing frame under construction around an X B R 500 cc Honda engine.*

Left *The complete Honda X B R-based machine.*

Opposite, right *The alloy chassis built for Steve Parish with the three Harris partners. From left to right: Steve Harris, Steve Bayford, Lester Harris.*

Opposite, left *The Parish frame in plan view.*

was much more difficult to carry out and, therefore, much more expensive.

Although the E M C based on the Harris Mk1 chassis was very competitive and successful, the formed Mk2 chassis produced even more success for the team, which went on to win two Isle of Man Trophy races with it. Harris produced approximately 12 Mk2 chassis for Dr Urlich to race under his E M C banner.

In 1984 the Formula 1 engine capacity was reduced from 1000 cc to 750 cc. Harris designed and built machines to race in this formula, and also ran a two-bike team under the Harris name, the riders being Asa Moyse and Jim Wells. Although faced by factory teams, the Harris team achieved sixth place in the World Championship that year.

On the whole, factory domination of Formula 1 was too strong for the private owners, which tended to spoil the formula somewhat. Despite this, the Harris machine proved popular with the private

teams, and approximately 50 were produced.

During the 1985 season, Harris ran a single-machine F1 team. The bike was built around a Kawasaki G B Z 750R engine, and was the first machine that Harris had built using a water-cooled, four-cylinder four-stroke. The rider was Asa Moyse.

Despite a sterling effort on Moyse's part, however, wins were not to come. The engine did not have the power output of the factory-backed adversaries. It was also too heavy, which had a serious effect on the power-to-weight ratio. The chassis design, on the other hand, proved popular with private teams and individuals, being seen as one of the best available. Something in the region of 35 were built, some having lighter, air-cooled engines.

In 1985 Harris also produced an alloy chassis that was based on a rectangular extrusion boxed in strategic areas to achieve the required structural performance. This housed a Yamaha R D L C 500 engine, a water-cooled, four-cylinder two-stroke.

Among the riders who chose this machine were Steve Parish, Ron Storey, Des Barry, Clive Paget and Phil Mellor.

Sadly, the RDLC 500 engine proved difficult to tune, while reliability was not its strong point. Consequently, a string of wins was not forthcoming.

In 1986 Harris made further improvements to the alloy-extrusion chassis for Steve Parish, who raced it with the Yamaha FZ 750 engine, also a water-cooled, four-cylinder four-stroke. This type of machine was also raced by Matt Oxley and Vesa Kultalahti in endurance events. The capability of this bike was indicated by the fact that they finished in a very creditable sixth place in the World Championship.

During 1986, Harris were contracted by Tetsu Ikuzawa of Japan to produce a bike and run it in the Suzuka eight-hour endurance race. They designed and built a chassis around the Honda VFR 750 engine, and the combination proved very competitive. The very prestigious endurance race attracted all the factory teams, who employed Grand Prix riders. However, the Harris entry, ridden by Trevor Nation, Graham McGregor and Ray Swan, ran in a very creditable seventh place until the closing stages when a pit-stop dropped them back. Despite this, they still finished in an excellent 12th place.

The following year, 1987, saw Harris building machines for the now-popular endurance racing formula. This led to the production of their first box-type chassis that was completely formed from alloy sheet. The lightweight, yet stiff, design was built around the Yamaha FZ 750 engine, although the same chassis was also made to accommodate the Kawasaki GPX 750.

The outstanding and advanced design was to finish second in that year's World Championship,

Above left An interesting project in 1986 was the 125 cc MBA. Alloy extrusions were used for the backbone-type frame.

Left The machine on Steve Parish's right is the complete alloy-chassis bike with the Yamaha FZ 750 engine. Harris undertook the complete project.

Top right A Mk2 Magnum in single-seat form.

Below right Two-seat version of the Mk2 Magnum.

while another example came fifth. This was an outstanding performance in the face of the full factory teams. The same design was modified to include the latest requirements for the 1988 endurance championship, and supplied to several private teams.

Earlier, 1986 had seen the inauguration of the Super Stock Formula, a series for production-based machines. The rules for Super Stock decreed the use of production chassis, but modifications were allowed as long as the general layout or appearance remained the same. This form of racing became popular quickly, and Harris soon found their experience and skills in demand. They carried out modifications to Suzuki, Yamaha and Kawasaki machines. Among the many riders to use Harris-

Top A 1988 F1 machine based on a Suzuki G S X R 750 cc engine.

Above This complete machine was built around a 900 cc Ducati engine.

Left Harris built a series of these machines for Laverda, the engine a 600 cc twin. During 1987, this machine was voted the best under-750 cc GT by Das Motorad magazine.

Above *Harris are prepared to go beyond pure engineering work, as this version of an aerodynamic fairing shows.*

Right *The Harris-modified Yamaha OWO1 for racing in the British National Championship.*

modified bikes were Keith Heuwen, Kenny Irons and Steve Parish.

Since the introduction of the Super Stock Formula, Harris have modified a large number of machines, and the work has become a steady business. At the time of writing, their skills are still much in demand.

During 1988, Harris developed another alloy chassis utilizing box-sections formed from alloy sheet. This chassis was for the S O S class, which was restricted to single-cylinder engines. Harris ran their own bike in this class, basing it on a Rotax 600 cc engine. It was ridden by Asa Moyse with great success: he won the British National Championship in 1989, and came second in 1990, although another Harris-framed bike did actually win the Championship.

The single-cylinder class of racing became popular very quickly, and Harris were called on to produce chassis for a number of privateers. In addition to the Rotax-engined type, versions were also produced for Honda and Yamaha engines.

For 1990, Harris sponsored an entry in the British Open Championship, the machine chosen

Left The Magnum Mk3, finished to a customer's specification.

Below This superb restoration of an M V Agusta demonstrates the versatility of Harris Performance Products.

Right The Harrier 3 uses a Harris frame designed for the Triumph triple.

being a Yamaha OWO1. The obligatory production chassis was modified in an effort to improve performance, while Mark Phillips was the rider.

During 1991, Harris became involved in an exciting project as a result of an approach by Yamaha, who offered to supply them with Grand Prix engines. Harris were to design and build the machines, which would be offered for sale to private buyers. This was a major step for an independent frame maker. The engines were Yamaha YZR 500 V4 two-strokes.

The frame designed to accommodate the Yamaha engine consisted of an aluminium delta box type with a carbon fibre seat sub-frame. The engine position was adjustable, as was the swinging rear fork spindle position. The front forks were Ohlins (upside-down type). Braking was taken care of by

AP six-piston calipers; the front brake disc was of carbon fibre, while the rear disc was steel. Marchesini wheels were fitted as standard, but carbon fibre wheels were offered as an option. This was all encapsulated in specially designed bodywork.

Six machines were built for the 1992 season, and all six went to private teams. However, the Padgets entry was supported by Harris. It was ridden by Simon Buckmaster.

For the 1993 season, Harris produced three machines. One was sold to a private entrant, but the remaining two were retained and run as a full works team sponsored by Shell. The riders were Sean Emmelt and Andrew Stroud.

The unique aspect of the Harris/Yamaha project is that it allows private teams to buy machines to complete at Grand Prix level. Moreover, they can opt for a service contract, which means that the bike will be serviced at all the race meetings by Harris technicians. This includes frame re-jigging and welding, along with comprehensive spares back-up, even to the extent of a spare engine should a customer suffer a catastrophic engine failure.

Since the advent of the Harris Grand Prix machines, they have put in some very creditable performances against the might of the factory teams, culminating in a sixth place in the 1992 British Grand Prix, ridden by Terry Rymer.

Although the results achieved in the first two seasons were not sensational, they have shown that an independent manufacturer can begin from scratch and produce competitive Grand Prix machinery. Harris have also shown the ability with their other products to improve performance, so the coming seasons will be interesting. The time may have come for the factory teams to sit up and take note.

Teamwork

Over the years, Harris Performance Products have designed and built machines for road and track in small numbers and large production runs. However, this has not been the sole aim of the business. To this day, they maintain their enthusiasm for designing and building prototypes, as well as making many engineering improvements and modifications, coupled with the occasional rebuild.

They have one major advantage in this business, in that most of the engineering processes required are available in-house. They employ top-class welders, fabricators and engineers, and they also have their own G R P shop, which means that all their bodywork can be made in-house. These facilities, together with their obvious engineering talents, have served them well and have led to the excellent reputation they enjoy world-wide.

There is one other ingredient that will keep Harris Performance Products in the forefront of independent motorcycle chassis builders for many years to come. That ingredient is enthusiasm, as strong now as it was in 1972, if not stronger.

The Harris story is one of many successes, but as can be imagined, on occasion those successes were gained the hard way, by mistakes and the inevitable things that went wrong. Fortunately, those occasions are few in number and haven't resulted in

memorable disasters. However, a few minor problems now raise a laugh; in their early days for instance they had built a chassis for a customer who wanted it nickel-plated. Harris arranged for this to be done, and the job was completed in time for them to spend the night building the bike into race trim, after which it was put straight into a crate for transit to an overseas race practice. Three days later, at the distant circuit, the rider and the owner waited for the bike to be unpacked, having spread the word about the new machine. Proud Harris personnel were on hand to accept any credit offered. But when the crate was opened, there was a stony silence. Inside, there was no gleaming nickel-plated racing chassis; instead, the bike was covered in what appeared to be a green fungus-like deposit. It was a memorable moment.

Another amusing episode is the time when the Harris team travelled to an overseas circuit with a

The Harris/Yamaha Grand Prix machine minus its bodywork.

van, a car and a caravan. As the caravan wasn't needed until they arrived, they had filled it completely with GRP fairings, which were to be sold from the paddock as a means of subsidizing the racing. The unfortunate driver towing the caravan did not know about the fairings until an officious customs officer pointed them out. The ensuing visit to the local cells is still laughed about, but the story didn't end there. On arrival at the circuit, they began to sell the fairings. At the time, these were unobtainable on the continent, so a good profit was considered possible. Since the cost was £15, a selling price of £30 was settled on. But a strange thing happened. Instead of selling individually, they began to sell in batches of ten or more. The mystery was solved later in the day, when it was discovered that the fairings were being re-sold for £60 each at stalls outside the paddock. Harris learnt a valuable lesson about market research that day.

Steve Bayford also recalls a funny moment, just after he joined Harris as a partner. A friend, who had been told that Steve was working for a company that made racing motorcycles, would phone him and open the conversation by saying: 'Barry Sheene here, can you make me a couple of bikes?' At the time, Barry Sheene was as big a name as possible in motorcycle racing, but Steve's unprintable reply always came quickly off the tongue. Then one day Steve picked up the phone and the voice said: 'Barry Sheene here. My bike won't handle. Would you consider building me one?' Steve's reply was: 'You can't handle your women, so I'm not surprised you can't handle your bike!' Fortunately, Mr Sheene took it in good part, and that call led to a long and successful association between the two.

6

IIIIIIII *Hejira Racing HRD*

Hejira is an unusual name for a very British business, but the translation explains all. 'Hejira' is Arabic for 'to fly', and the performance record of the machines from this company justifies its title.

Hejira design and manufacture racing motorcycle frames, and have chosen to concentrate in this area. However, some of their frames, built to house larger engines, have been utilized in the construction of road machines.

The man behind Hejira, Derek Chittenden, was born with competition blood coursing through his veins. His father was an avid grass track racer, and Derek followed in his father's footsteps, although his will to compete took him into other forms of motorcycle sport. One that he pursued very strongly was motocross, then he took to road racing. Maintaining the family tradition, his eldest son now designs and builds Hejiras, while his youngest son has taken up motocross.

Derek Chittenden's competitive spirit made him reluctant to drop one type of racing to pursue another. In fact, his experiences on one Bank Holiday weekend are unlikely to be equalled by many people, and rarely beaten. He competed in a grass track meeting on the Friday, took part in a road race on the Saturday, then competed in a motocross meeting on the Monday – not bad for an amateur club competitor.

Motocross was the sport on which Derek began to concentrate, however, and the more involved he became, the more he found the need to have equipment built to suit his personal needs. This is where his engineering skills, gained through an apprenticeship with British Rail, proved to be more than useful. Derek had carried out the inevitable modifications to existing machines which, in turn, led to the manufacture of a complete motocross frame. This was built during 1960. Over the next few years, more motocross frames were built, as other riders wanted to benefit from his skills. A lot of experience was gained in building these frames. Then, in 1974, Derek took a significant step by building his first road race frame. This housed a

Above *Derek Chittenden, in 1977, on a bike based on one of his own Hejira motocross frames. During this early period, motocross was Derek's favoured sport; road racing was to come later.*

Above right *The first prototype road racing frame built by Derek Chittenden at the end of 1973. It housed a 250 cc Ducati engine. Although bearing the Hejira name, it was actually built before the company had been formed.*

Right *A 1979 Hejira road racing frame for 250 and 350 cc engines. Note the use of round steel tubing.*

250 cc Ducati engine, and it was built for a rider who had the good sense to feel that Derek's skill should be extended beyond motocross frames.

That first road race frame lived up to expectations and resulted in orders for further examples. In fact, during 1975, Derek built four. Again, these machines utilized the 250 cc Ducati engine. Together with some friends, Derek ran two of these bikes as a team. Two seasons later, in 1977, he built four more road race frames. Each housed an AJS 250 cc Stormer engine, a two-stroke single.

The amazing thing about Derek Chittenden's frame building is, at that point in his career, all the work had been carried out as a hobby on a part-time basis. He even found time to compete on motorcycles himself. However, the time had come to decide what to do about this time-consuming hobby.

The frames he had built had performed well in Clubman racing. This produced a growing reputation, which led to a demand for frames from other enthusiasts. As as result, Derek decided to turn his hobby into a full-time business.

Thus, in 1978, Hejira Racing H R D Ltd was born. Derek had chosen the company name several years before, and all the machines he had built prior to that date had carried the Hejira name. Consequently, a useful reputation had been built up on which the company could begin to trade.

In fact, the new company was a partnership

between Derek Chittenden and Danny Wilson. However, in 1989, ill health caused Danny to pull out of Hejira, and he went his own way.

The first frame built by the new company housed a 250 cc twin-cylinder Suzuki engine. This led to further work in the 250 cc class, a very competitive formula that lends itself to frame development. Derek Chittenden's experience and proven ability made him a prime candidate to fill the needs of the competitors in this area.

The small company soon became very busy, designing and building frames for Suzuki, Yamaha, Rotax and Sach engines, all of them racing 250s. In fact, in this outstanding season, Hejira built over 30 racing frames, a lot of machines in racing terms. This type of work continued over the next two seasons, mainly for the 250 cc racing formula.

Up to this point, all the frames designed and built by Derek Chittenden utilized round steel tubing,

Far left, below The development prototype of the hub-centre steering machine.

Below left Richard Hunter on a 1982 Hejira Suzuki. Richard finished in an excellent second place in the F3 T T on the Isle of Man.

Left Steve Cull on a 600 cc Hejira Ducati during the 1983–4 season. He finished ninth in the F2 race on the Isle of Man.

Right A serious-looking Derek Chittenden is shown with a Hejira Ducati in 1984.

but during 1981, the transition to square-section steel tubing took place. Derek advocates the use of steel tubing when conventional methods of frame making are employed. Apart from the change to square-section tubing, his method of frame manufacture has remained the same for 30 years. Obviously, it was right in the first place.

All the frames designed and built by this company have their own design of swinging rear fork, again built from welded steel tubing. As each rear fork is designed to meet the specific needs of the frame, the section of the tubing used will be selected to achieve the required performance. Front forks usually come from a major fork manufacturer, selected to achieve the best results. Years of racing, building and preparing competition bikes has given Derek Chittenden a wealth of experience when it comes to selecting the most advantageous components, such as shock absorbers, brakes, electrics and all the parts necessary to achieve the maximum possible engine performance. Like most race bike builders, Derek Chittenden has considerable expertise in the last area, particularly the all-important exhaust system.

In 1982 Hejira widened their horizons when they built their first frame for a Rotax 500 cc single. It led to further orders for this type of frame, as the single-cylinder formula was gaining popularity.

Although still a comparatively small company, they entered into a busy programme of building racing frames for the 250 and 500 cc single formulae. Despite this, they also managed to produce frame designs for other engines and formulae. Frames were built to house engines from 750 to 1100 cc. In the main, these were four-cylinder

powerplants from Suzuki, Kawasaki and Honda. Most of these machines were built for the various formulae operated at national club level, but some frames were supplied to customers who completed their machines for road use.

It would have appeared that this energetic and enthusiastic frame maker had enough to keep him busy, having established a wide base of capabilities to ensure continued business. However, Derek Chittenden was about to surprise the motorcycling fraternity with another innovative project.

During 1983, on top of all the other Hejira work, he designed and built a complete machine that featured hub-centre steering. Although it was not the first hub-centre steering frame ever produced, it was certainly a bold and advanced project for such a small company.

Unlike some hub-centre steering projects, which used the engine as a stressed member of the frame, the Hejira version had a full centre section. In other words, it was a complete rolling chassis even without the engine. One major advantage of this arrangement was that the chassis could be made to accept almost any engine, or range of engines.

Derek Chittenden's design utilized square-section steel tubing in the construction of the frame and the upper front suspension wishbone. Larger rectangular sections were used for the single leading leg of the front suspension, and for the conventional Hejira swinging rear forks.

Sheet steel was employed to fabricate a large, deep-section backbone for the frame. Another interesting aspect of this machine was its fabricated front wheel. This was designed and made by Hejira to meet the need for an offset wheel to accommodate the single-leg front suspension.

The wheel consisted of a steel disc centre, bolted to a flanged rim. To achieve the offset, long spacers were fitted between the rim flange and the centre. A large-diameter, single front brake disc was mounted within the offset wheel. As a conventional swinging rear fork was used, the rear wheel was a normal off-the-shelf item.

Many test miles were covered by this interesting prototype, but the lack of a development budget prevented its potential from being established. However, this prototype is still retained by Hejira and may be developed further if resources allow, or its technology may be utilized for other machines in the future.

Over the next few seasons, Hejira continued to construct the frames on which they had built their reputation, as well as making continual modifications to customer's machines. On top of this, they ran a works racing team in the singles formula. In 1986 the engine size for this formula was raised from 500 to 600 cc, although this didn't necessitate any change to the frame design.

In 1991 another advanced design was under way at Hejira. For this project, Derek Chittenden was investigating the potential of the very latest in materials technology.

The new design was for a frame and swinging rear fork to be built taking full advantage of modern composites. Carbon fibre was utilized as the main structural material for both the frame and rear fork,

Above *A typical range of steel frames offered by Hejira. This style of construction has been used from 1986 to the time of writing. Note the change to square-section steel tubing.*

Top *Left to right: Derek Chittenden, Martin Bartlett (the rider), Danny Wilson (Derek's partner in the early years of Hejira). The machine is a Hejira 250 twin. This photograph was taken in 1986, during the British Championship round at Silverstone.*

Right *By 1992, Hejira were using advanced technology to produce this carbon fibre frame and rear fork. The machine, which was equipped with a 600 cc Rotax engine, was raced by the company.*

while some aerospace-type honeycomb was used strategically to enhance the performance in specific areas. This exciting project was a joint effort between Derek Chittenden and Max Powell. Derek's experience of what was required from the frame was fulfilled by Max, who took care of the composite design.

The resultant frame was of a backbone type except that, unlike the normal twin-spar layout, the spar sides were joined together at the rear in similar fashion to the steering head area. Integral extensions carried the swinging rear fork pivots.

To achieve this very impressive arrangement, carbon fibre prepreg materials, suitable for the structural requirements, were moulded at elevated temperature under vacuum. Carbon fibre materials were moulded in the same way to produce the all-composite swinging rear fork. Bearing housings, such as those for the steering head and the swinging rear fork, were machined metallic components bonded onto the moulded carbon fibre parts as a secondary operation.

Composites have many advantages over conventional materials in the manufacture of structural components such as motorcycle frames. In most cases, weight can be saved while still obtaining the required structural performance. This can be achieved by the selection of specific materials, and enhanced in specific areas by orientation of the fibres for maximum strength. Extra material need only be added where more strength is required. In this way, structural performance can be optimized without the addition of unwanted weight.

Designing and manufacturing in composite materials are somewhat different to working with conventional materials. Varying performances can be achieved with the same material, depending on the method which is used. Therefore, composite structures are more individuated than structures made from conventional materials, which is why there is no detailed technical information on the Hejira carbon fibre frame. However, it is very much stiffer than the steel tubing frame that is being run on a second bike and serves as the comparison. The added bonus is that it is of course lighter in weight than the steel tubing frame.

400 flyers

From the very beginning, Hejira have chosen to remain a small company, but they are big in enthusiasm, skill and innovation. They have concentrated on racing frames, although some have been prepared as road machines by customers. Those used on the track, however, have been successful in various formulae, for both Hejira customers and the company's works entries. The list of victories gained by Hejira-framed machines is very impressive.

Since production commenced, Hejira have produced over 400 race frames. Throughout, they have adopted an innovative and bold approach to motorcycle frame making. At the time of writing, they are still producing race frames, and running their own race team. You can be sure that whatever comes next from Derek Chittenden and Hejira will work, and work well, in true Hejira tradition.

7

▮▮▮▮▮▮ *Magni*

Magni are well known in the motorcycle world for two good reasons: their connections with one of the world's most famous motorcycle factories, MV Agusta, and the excellent reputation they have achieved for the exciting motorcycles they have produced in their own right.

The company's founder, Arturo Magni, had what can only be described as a dream start to his career with motorcycles. This came about in 1947, when he joined the racing department of Gilera. During this period, he was involved in the assembly of the famous Gilera four-cylinder engines. This background was to prove invaluable. To extend this experience even further, he moved to MV Agusta, taking up a position in their racing department.

Arturo Magni eventually became chief of the MV Agusta racing department and remained in this position until MV withdrew from racing. He was responsible for motorcycles raced by the most famous riders of that period, admired to this day, such as Agostini, Surtees and Hailwood. To give an indication of the challenge laid down by the combination of these riders and MV Agusta machines, when the MV factory ceased racing they had won 75 world championships.

The experience gained over 20 years in some of the world's greatest racing departments was too valuable an asset to waste, so in 1977 a factory was opened by Arturo Magni and his sons, who set about building a family business in the world of motorcycling. In the beginning, the new business produced special parts for MV Agusta machines, such as chain transformation kits, cylinder and piston kits, fairings, saddles, and special exhaust systems. After a comparatively short time, they designed and began to manufacture the first frame to bear the Magni name. This was designed to house the four-cylinder MV Agusta engine, which is not surprising considering the connections at hand.

This vast experience and skill resulted in Magni producing parts for the four-cylinder MV engine. These enabled enthusiasts to restore four-cylinder MVs, and even build copies of the MV Agusta racing bike.

A few years later, Magni produced the first complete motorcycle to bear their name. This machine was based on the 900 cc four-cylinder Honda Bol d'Or engine. Two versions were produced: the MH1 and MH2. The former utilized some of the original Honda parts, such as wheels and front

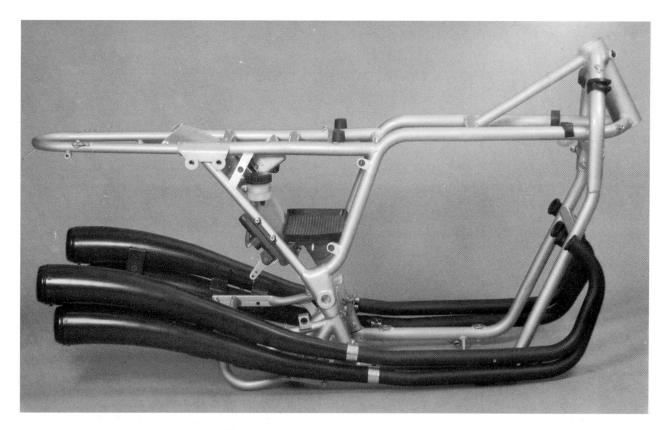

Below left An example of the first complete motorcycle produced by Magni: the M H 1. A Honda 900 cc four-cylinder engine is utilized, along with the donor bike's front forks and wheels. The M H 2 made use of the engine alone and was fitted with a full fairing.

Below An early 1980s M B 2 with a 1000 cc B M W boxer engine.

Above All the early frames built by the company were similar to this example, which is designed to accept a four-cylinder MV Agusta unit.

forks. This model was also supplied without a fairing. The M H 2 was a complete machine with a full fairing and using only the engine from the original Honda motorcycle. It proved very popular, somewhere in the region of 300 being produced.

During 1982–3, Magni designed and built a new frame to house a totally different type of engine: the 1000 cc B M W Boxer. Again, two versions were available, one being a basic model designated the M B 1, the other (the M B 2) being the top-of-the-range model. The latter had all the Magni-manufactured components, including a full fairing set.

Right *Magni Le Mans, first seen at the Milan show in November 1985, with a choice of 948 or 1116 cc Moto Guzzi engines. The first Magni machine offered complete and not as a frame kit.*

Above left *Magni's parallelogram rear suspension system. This provided shaft drive with the feel of a normal chain drive by eliminating the transmission reactions. Other manufacturers have since copied this idea.*

Left *The left-side view of the parallelogram suspension.*

Above *Although marketed in 1987, the Classico was built with 1970s styling. It proved a popular model.*

Although this proved a popular machine, Magni were only able to produce about 150 examples, because BMW introduced the K-series, and the Boxer engine went out of production.

From the very beginning, Magni have continually strived to give the customers what they want. Hence continual changes in styling, as well as technical advances. An example of this awareness of what is needed is the Le Mans model, introduced during the first half of the 1980s. It boasted a full fairing of modern design, similar in style to the big-selling Japanese machines, while the technical specification was similarly up to date, particularly in the use of a parallelogram rear suspension system. This arrangement, designed by Magni, gave the machine a completely new feel. All the transmission reactions were eliminated, the shaft-drive system having the feel of a normal chain-driven transmission. Other motorcycle manufacturers have since utilized this system.

In 1987 the company chased the market with two new models: the Classico and the Arturo. Again, these were examples of Magni's innovation, although the styles were reminiscent of motorcycles of the 1970s. They had spoked wheels, 1970s-style mudguards, large round headlights, and a lack of bodywork, except in the case of the Arturo, which had a small half fairing.

Although the machines appeared to be a retrograde step in motorcycle terms, their 1970s styling proved very popular, especially when built to the usual Magni high standard, all the components and accessories being of the very best quality.

The success of the Classico and Arturo models led Magni into taking the theme even further when, in 1989, they produced the SFIDA, which was designed in the style of 1960s motorcycles. Again, spoked wheels were used, and aluminium fuel tanks of the period were reproduced. This model was produced as a single-seater.

The SFIDA is still being produced at the time of writing, and over 500 examples have been sold. Also, Magni are still producing the Arturo, but now it is offered with the latest Moto Guzzi engine, which has four valves per cylinder. This is yet another example of Magni's efforts to offer the best.

The very latest model produced by Magni is the Australia. This is a race-styled motorcycle sold for road use. Its styling is up to the minute, while its performance matches the looks.

Power and style

Magni have established a reputation for producing top-class and exciting motorcycles, both for race and road use. This has resulted in the company's recent success.

The business has been built on giving the motorcycle world what it wants in terms of performance, styling and quality of build. All Magni tubular frames are built from 25 CROMO 4 tubing, argon welding being used to achieve the required structural performance. The number of machines that have been built since the company began gives a good indication of the quality of design and manufacture.

As shown by this account, Magni have striven to keep ahead of what the public want, and it is likely that they will continue to do so. Motorcycling enthusiasts can look forward to many more exciting models from this Italian company. Despite their forward-thinking approach, however, if a customer has an M V Agusta four-cylinder engine, Magni will build a racing lookalike. That's long-term customer service at its best.

Below left *An example of the S F I D A. This particular version utilizes a 1000 cc Moto Guzzi engine.*

Below *The Australia model in full race trim. Both Australia models make use of the 1000 cc Guzzi engine.*

CHAPTER
8
■■■■■■ Maxton Engineering

Maxton Engineering and Ron Williams are one and the same, and need little or no introduction in the competition motorcycle world, having designed and built a wide range of racing motorcycle chassis for a variety of users, including factory teams. He is a very talented designer and builder of racing motorcycle chassis and suspensions.

Ron Williams left school at 16 and began an engineering apprenticeship. When this training was completed, he became a draughtsman with A E I. In 1966, with experience added to his engineering training, he joined Chevron Cars as their chief draughtsman.

During his time with Chevron Cars, Ron designed single-seater and sports car chassis for a variety of formulae, including F3 and F5000. These cars made use of such engines as Cosworth and BMW.

All his technical knowledge and practical experience, coupled with a love of competition motorcycles, led Ron into building and racing his own sprint machine in his spare time. This was a successful venture, and he took several world records for both standing and flying start.

During this very busy period, Ron had also become very interested in suspension systems. This led to the design and construction of a shock absorber testing machine for Chevron. The motorcycle bug appeared again, however: incorporated in

Left An example of the machines built by Maxton for the Dugdale team.

Top The first cantilever frame built by Maxton Engineering in 1975. This was to prove very successful for them.

Above This Maxton machine has been fitted with an extra-large fuel tank so that it can complete four full laps of the Isle of Man. It was ridden by Steve Carthy.

this machine was a Norton gearbox.

Although engaged on competition car work, Ron was becoming increasingly interested in the new breed of motorcycle coming into England, powered by two-stroke engines. His interest was heightened by the problems the new type of engine brought with it. Handling and reliability were serious problems, associated in many cases with vibration caused by the high-revving two-strokes. The challenge they offered was too great to resist, and in 1971, after five years with Chevron, Ron resigned. He had decided to design and manufacture frames to house these new and exciting engines.

The workshop for Ron's enterprise was the garage attached to his parents' house. During his first year, he built six frames of steel tubing construction, and the success of these first six was evident. The very next year, he built over 20 frames, and this level of production was maintained for some years after. It was an impressive output when you consider that he did not employ anyone. He carried out all the main construction work, only a minimum of work being subcontracted out.

After a few years, Ron was able to purchase a disused Methodist chapel, which was turned into a purpose-built workshop. This was to become the home of the now well known Maxton Engineering.

During this period, all the frames from Maxton Engineering were of steel tubing construction, designed and built by Ron Williams himself. In addition to the many frames for clubmen riders, he also built machines for riders of great experience, who were competing all over the world.

Maxton built chassis for 250 and 350 cc grand prix machines, in addition to examples for the Isle of Man TT races and the Manx races. During 1975, Maxton supplied chassis for Dugdale the motorcycle dealers, to race in the Manx GP series. Their confidence in Maxton Engineering and Ron Williams was to prove extremely rewarding, for their team went on to win all the Manx races at 250, 350 and 500 cc.

This success is proof of Ron Williams' skill, but what makes it even more outstanding is that the same chassis design was used in all three classes, a rare feat indeed. Credit must also be given to Dugdale's preparation and running of the team.

The list of riders of Maxton machines is almost endless, but at this stage of the company's history it

Various stages in the construction of the frame built by Ron Williams to house the Honda NR 500 oval-piston engine. This was constructed in the UK and shipped to Japan for evaluation.

Top *The second chassis for the N R 500 engine. This example was built at the Honda works, but under the supervision of Ron Williams.*

Above *The complete N R 500 racer.*

included such riders as Chris Mortimer, Tom Herron, John Williams, Charlie Williams, Bernard Murray, Tony Rutter, Steve Parish, Eddie Roberts, Stan Woods, Roger Marshall and Steve Machin.

At the time, a large percentage of the frames produced were for Yamaha 125, 250 and 350 cc engines. However, frames were also made to take Ducati Pantah engines. This work was carried out for Sports Motorcycles, who had Tony Rutter to ride their machines. Earlier, in 1974, Maxton Engineering took a significant step by working for Suzuki. This collaboration with a major Japanese manufacturer illustrates the respect in which the skills of Ron Williams and Maxton Engineering were held.

The work included a chassis which, in essence, was a forerunner of the R G 500. This machine was raced by Paul Smart in the 1974 British Grand Prix, followed by the remainder of the world's G Ps that year.

Maxton also built frames for C Z, which were raced by Eddie Roberts and Dave Hickman. Then, during the late 1970s, Ron Williams went to work for another major manufacturer when he built a special chassis for Yamaha. This housed a three-cylinder, 500 cc engine, and was ridden by the Japanese works rider, Takasumi Katayama.

A major advance, which was instrumental in keeping Maxton Engineering among the leading independent chassis makers, came about in 1975 when they built their first cantilever machine. This particular chassis housed a 350 cc engine, and the machine was an instant success. Ridden by Charlie Williams, it won the Isle of Man Junior T T.

Continued success added to the excellent reputation of Ron Williams and Maxton Engineering. Frames were still being manufactured in the converted chapel, and the company's output included machines for Formula 1. Some of these were based on Suzuki engines, while others utilized Honda powerplants.

For 1980, an interesting step was taken with the production of a road bike, which was to be the first and only road machine produced by Maxton. This one-off, designed and built by Ron Williams himself, used a conventional steel tubing chassis and housed an L C 350 Yamaha engine. Also at this time, another new chassis was designed and built, but this one was to change the direction of Ron Williams' career.

Ron had been approached by the research and development department of Honda to build a chassis for the N R 500 four-stroke. This engine was the revolutionary oval-piston G P project. On accepting the project, he was supplied with a sample engine around which he was to build the chassis. This was of steel tubing construction. With most new designs, a constructor likes to maintain at least some degree of confidentiality until ready to unveil

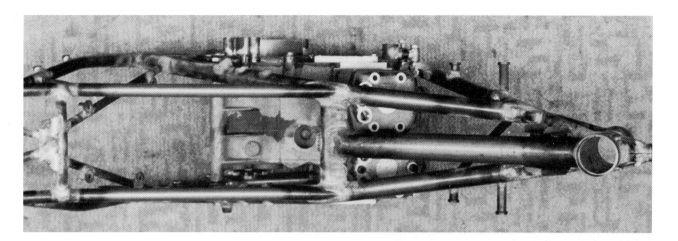

A steel-tubing frame built around a C Z engine. The finished machine was raced by Dave Hickman and Eddie Roberts.

his work, but with this project Honda insisted that the work be carried out under conditions of utmost secrecy.

When the machine was complete, it was shipped to Honda in Japan, where a full working engine was fitted and a test programme started. Ron Williams' work must have impressed, as he was asked by the team manager of the Honda International Racing Corporation to fly to Japan to assist in the development programme and test work, with the possibility of becoming a consultant to the Honda racing team.

After a visit to the Honda factory, where terms were agreed, Ron became an official consultant to the research and development department. In this new position, he set about building four more chassis. However, this time, all the construction work was carried out by Japanese personnel; Ron was to carry out the design work and then oversee the actual manufacture.

So that he could devote sufficient time to this project, Ron scaled down his frame production to a few one-offs that could be built during the closed season. By now, he was travelling the world as a race technician with the Honda G P Team.

During the early 1980s, the closed-season period

Above left *A Maxton-built steel-tubing chassis for the 1983 MCN Superbike series.*

Left *The swinging rear fork for the Superbike chassis. The finished machine was ridden by Ron Haslam and Wayne Gardner.*

Above right *A cantilever chassis for a 500 cc, single-cylinder engine. It was built during 1984.*

Right *Maxton took another step forward in 1985, when they produced their first formed-aluminium, twin-spar frame.*

enabled Ron to produce some of his famous designs, one of which showed that Maxton Engineering were keeping up with modern trends. This was his first deltabox design, that is a twin-spar chassis in which the main members are made from formed aluminium sheet, welded together to form deep box-like sections. This construction, although new in both design and materials, was still made completely by Maxton in their factory. Three of these aluminium deltabox chassis were made, all to house 250 cc engines.

In addition to the alloy frames produced for solo machines, Ron Williams designed and built a sidecar chassis. Again, this was diversification, in two respects. One was that Maxton Engineering had never built a sidecar chassis before; the other was the unfamiliar method of construction, being a stressed-skin aluminium monocoque riveted and glued together. This machine was powered by a TZ 750 Yamaha engine.

The 1980s saw Maxton Engineering continue to make technical advances. One notable innovation was achieved in the form of two composite chassis. These machines were designed and built by Ron

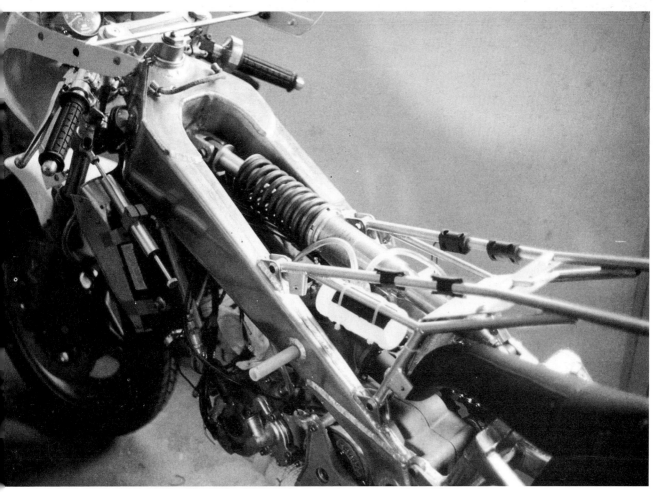

Williams in his Maxton Engineering factory, and made use of moulded carbon and Kevlar fibres. Having made his own moulds, he used the wet lay-up method to produce the laminated chassis members, assembling the two chassis completely in-house.

Originally, the composite chassis were produced to house 250 cc Honda and Yamaha engines, but later one was fitted and raced with a 350 cc Yamaha engine. Composite technology is vastly different in both design and manufacturing methods to conventional motorcycle frame materials. These two frames illustrated the skill and versatility of Maxton Engineering.

During the mid 1980s, Ron Williams still managed to produce a small number of steel tubing chassis to take single-cylinder 500 and 600 cc four-stroke engines. By that time, this form of racing had become very popular.

He was to make 1987 his last year of working with a Grand Prix team. This last season was spent with Rothman's International, whose rider was Roger Burnett. In previous years, on the Grand Prix scene with Honda, he worked with riders such as Mick Grant, Takasumi Katayama, Wayne Gardner, Roger Marshall, Roger Burnett, Ron Haslam, Joey Dunlop and Richard Scott.

With his globe-trotting days behind him, Ron decided to develop his business again, but not in the manufacture of frames. Instead, he embarked on a completely new venture: the manufacture of mgnesium wheels. With design and development carried out in true Maxton tradition, a three-spoke magnesium motorcycle wheel went into production in 1988.

During 1989, Ron Williams became aware that there was a strong demand from riders who wanted the means to convert their road bikes for racing, and two areas of motorcycle engineering of particular interest to him were front forks and rear

Left *A further advance was made by Ron Williams when he produced this carbon fibre composite chassis. The use of this totally different technology demonstrates the innovative thinking behind the company.*

Above *Maxton have not restricted their work purely to two-wheeled machines, as this sheet-aluminium sidecar chassis shows.*

Right *The rarest of all Maxton machines: the only road bike ever built by the company.*

suspensions. As a result, a business was built around the conversion and supply of these components. This has led to Maxton Engineering becoming a service centre for Koni, a major manufacturer of suspension components.

By 1990, the lure of racing was too much for Ron Williams, so he moved back into the racing business, working for the ill-starred John Player Norton racing team. In 1991, he had returned to his great love, designing.

The Williams touch

Over the years, Maxton Engineering and Ron Williams have shown great capability and versatility. The list of riders, many of them famous, who have benefited from the skill and dedication shown by Maxton, in supplying the right equipment at the right time, must be long indeed.

∎∎∎∎∎ P & M Motorcycles

This well known British manufacturer of racing motorcycle frames used to be known, and will be remembered by some, as Peckett and McNab. That was the original name of the company when it was formed in 1975 by Richard Peckett and Peter McNab.

Richard and Peter met three years prior to forming the company, while working together at Dresda Autos. This employment must have given both of them invaluable experience, which was to be utilized to the full when they began designing and building motorcycle frames, or modifying existing ones.

Peckett and McNab was formed on capital raised

Below An early example of Peckett and McNab's engineering skills. This frame was built in 1976 to house a BMW twin. It was raced in endurance events by Richard Peckett and Denis McMillan, achieving a sixth place at Zandvoort.

Right A 1979 machine with a 998 cc Kawasaki engine. It was designed and built to race in F1 events.

Below right P & M built their first road bike in 1980, and this is the first example. The frame held a Kawasaki Z1R engine, bored out to 1100 cc, which produced phenomenal performance. Unfortunately, it was written off quite early by a P & M employee.

by Richard when he sold his Trident, which he had built while working at Dresda Autos, and Peter who sold his Rob North Triple. With the proceeds, they were able to move into premises in Arragon Street, Twickenham, on 1st November 1975.

In fact, the company's new home was an old builder's yard, but Richard had had some carpentry experience, while a relative was an electrician, so the workshop was soon renovated. Some cheap, secondhand machinery saw the company underway.

For a company aiming to manufacture and modify racing motorcycle frames, it had a great asset in that the partners were both motorcyclists. Richard, being a serious race rider, was and still is in the position to know what is required from a new build, and what modifications are required to an existing machine. This knowledge was to prove invaluable over the coming years.

During the early part of the company's existence, almost any engineering jobs were undertaken to get the business going. A Dresda Honda, owned by Richard, was dismantled and the frame was sold. Then, in the evenings when the day's moneymaking work was done, Richard and Peter designed and built a frame to house the Honda engine.

The new machine, which was race prepared for the 1976 season, was their very first, the P & M 1. Unfortunately, on the second lap of the first practice with this machine, the primary chain broke and wrecked the engine. It was rebuilt, and the machine ran on until the end of the season.

That first machine was given a new engine for the 1977 season. On its first outing, the Transatlantic Meeting at Brands Hatch, it won the four-stroke race and finished eighth in the MCN Superbike race, ridden on both occasions by Richard Peckett himself. More wins followed at club and national events, including a second place at a British Championship meeting. This performance from their first frame was a very good advertisement for the potential capabilities of the new company.

The second frame built by Peckett and McNab housed a BMW twin engine, and was ridden in endurance events by Richard Peckett and Denis Macmillan. The last recorded result for this combination of machine and riders was a sixth place at Zandvoort in 1977.

Both partners were still keeping the company going by undertaking any work that came along, but in the evenings, they spent extra hours making jigs and fixtures for producing all the parts that go with a motorcycle frame. All this was in preparation for the production of frames in a professional manner, when the opportunity came their way.

Between other work, frames three and four were designed and built. The former housed a Suzuki 500 cc twin, while the latter held a Kawasaki. Richard rode the Kawasaki himself and reports that it was very quick. Various engine problems needed attention, however, such as the fitting of an oil cooler, while regular engine seizing was overcome by fitting a different make of piston. As a matter of interest, this Kawasaki is still being raced at the time of writing, illustrating the soundness of the design and manufacture.

Left The second road bike utilized many parts salvaged from the original. It is still with its original owner and sees regular use.

Right A typical P & M chassis being built.

Below right The rising-rate rear suspension arrangement under construction.

The original Honda was still being raced by the company, but they decided to build a new frame for it. Asa Moyse rode the resultant machine in the first ever Formula One short-circuit race at Silverstone, while Richard Peckett rode the Kawasaki. From the start, Richard held second place to Ron Haslam, but he was soon passed by Alistair Frane. The next few laps saw a close battle with Roger Nichols, but this came to an end when they collided passing a back marker.

The company were taking their racing very seriously, as it was sensibly considered good advertising for their capabilities. To this end, they decided to build a new frame for the Kawasaki.

An interesting race for Peckett and McNab took place at the last Brands Hatch meeting of 1977. Richard Peckett rode the re-framed Kawasaki, Asa Moyse borrowed the old Kawasaki frame, and John Cowie rode the Honda, while the London distributor Mocheck borrowed the old Honda frame. This resulted in the front row of the grid having two works Hondas and four Peckett and McNab machines. The two works Hondas came first and sixth, while Peckett and McNab machines were second, third, fourth and fifth. This was an excellent result for the newly-formed company and was, without doubt, responsible for putting them on the map, generating orders for machines for the new F1 series.

Mocheck ordered two machines, Jim Wells and Tony Osborne one each, while more orders came in from other riders. This got the 1978 season off to an excellent start. To add to their racing commitment, an agreement was made to supply a chassis for John Cowie and Bernie Toleman to ride in endurance races. The engine and running expenses for this were to be provided by Albion Street Motors, in whose colours the machine would run.

The first meeting for the endurance machine was at Le Mans, where it finished a very creditable third. This excellent placing at an important venue

drew attention to the machine, and an offer of help came from Girling, whose rear shock absorbers were being used. At this point, the agreement with Albion Street Motors came to an early end, and the machine ran in the Peckett and McNab red and white colour scheme for the rest of the season.

P & M were kept busy, as John Cowie wanted to compete in the new F1 series as well as in endurance racing. They were constantly changing the machine from one spec. to the other. As well as supplying Steve Manship with an F1 Kawasaki, the company also ran a third machine for Richard Peckett himself. However, 1978 was not a good riding season for Richard. He suffered a broken shoulder-blade at the beginning of the season, and never seemed to get it together after that. Almost certainly, his workload prevented him from giving his riding its usual effort.

Despite Richard's problems, 1978 was a very good year for the company, both from the amount

of business transacted and results from company-supported machinery. The highlight was John Cowie winning the F1 championship, while another high point was when he won at Silverstone, beating Tom Herron and Mike Hailwood in the process.

The big win at Silverstone was not without some drama, as John Cowie's machine was a candidate for disqualification. At the time, the rules stated that all engines must use standard carburettors and that no major welding was allowed to crankcases. As the Peckett and McNab machine also served as an endurance racer, the oil filler aperture in the crankcase had been machined to accept a large-bore alloy tube, which had been welded in with an adaptor to prevent oil from contaminating the clutch. This gave no technical advantage whatsoever, and only served to assist filling during endurance events. In the F1 race, the fuel and oil were put in prior to the race. Moreover, it was pointed out that the crankcases of Mike Hailwood's machine had considerable welding modifications to fit certain parts.

In addition to the modified crankcase, P & M's machine was also claimed to have bored-out carburettors, the bore being measured at 28·5 mm

Above *One of P & M's last F1 machines, a 750 cc, receives attention from its creator, Richard Peckett.*

Below right *Richard Peckett demonstrating his riding skills on a machine designed and built by himself. His riding ability has served him well in determining just what is required to get the best from a machine.*

instead of the regulation 28 mm. It was pointed out to the scrutineer that the carburettors were as purchased with the engine. Some brand-new carburettors were located and measured; they, too, were 28·5 mm. Then it was discovered that they were being measured in the wrong place. Measured correctly, they were of the required 28 mm bore, so John Cowie was the confirmed winner.

Honda borrowed a Peckett and McNab chassis for Ron Haslam to ride in the last F1 meeting of the season, at Brands Hatch. In winning the race, he set a lap record that was to stand for several seasons. This was excellent testimony to the abilities of the company as motorcycle chassis builders.

As well as the excellent performance from Peckett and McNab machines during this first season of the new F1 series, their bikes produced some notable performances in endurance racing, including a third at Le Mans, a fourth at Spa, twelfth at the Bol d'Or, and sixth and seventh places at Brands Hatch. Among a series of good performances, there are usually times when things don't go to plan, and Peckett and McNab were no exceptions to this rule. Their machine suffered a crash at the Nürburgring, and an engine seizure in Barcelona.

Due to the engine seizure, some hurried work was put in at P & M to rebuild the engine for the Race of Aces meeting at Snetterton that coming weekend. This rebuild was completed on the Saturday afternoon, and the engine put into the bike to leave for Snetterton that very evening. An unnamed member of the crew, who stopped the transporter at about midnight, removed the bike from the back and, using the endurance lights, rode it the last 97 km (60 miles) to Snetterton to run in the new engine.

All this effort proved justified, for despite falling from a 125 cc Honda in an earlier race and being badly bruised, John Cowie went on to win the race for Peckett and McNab from Phil Read. This type

of performance was surely not going unnoticed. By this time, Dunlop were supplying the team with tyres of the same specification as those supplied to the top riders.

In addition to Dunlop's recognition, in the winter of 1978–9, the team were asked by Honda if they would be interested in running Honda-powered bikes for the 1979 season. The deal was that P & M would receive help from Gilberts of Catford, and Honda would loan three race-prepared engines. These were to be based on the CB 900 that was due out at that time. The offer was accepted, two machines being built for Roger Marshall and Tony Rutter. Honda also ordered a rolling chassis for their works team. As it turned out, the chassis supplied to Honda Britain from Japan were good, so the P & M frame was not used.

A Peckett and McNab machine was ridden during the season by Alex George, who achieved some good results. Normally, this machine would have been ridden by Richard Peckett himself, but he was taking a sabbatical to get married. During this period, Peter McNab looked after the racing side of the business.

Above Left-side view of the current P & M classic racer, the Trident.

Left Right-side view of the Trident.

Below right This fine action shot shows Richard Peckett racing his own Trident in one of the popular classic events.

At the end of 1979, Peter announced that he wanted to leave the business. Richard Peckett was prepared to purchase his share, and by the following October they had parted company. Richard decided to rename the company P & M Motorcycles, as by now their machines had become known as P & Ms, so the new abbreviated title seemed appropriate.

Peter McNab didn't get away from P & M machines completely, however, as a gentleman by the name of George Beale bought two of them. Peter went to work for his team, running the two machines for riders Roger Marshall and Graham Macgregor.

During 1980, P & M were to take a step in another direction. This was to produce a road machine. This first road bike utilized a secondhand ZIR Kawasaki engine, bored out to 1100 cc. It was road-tested by most of the leading motorcycle magazines and, in all cases, the reports were full of praise. In fact, one magazine was very reluctant to return the machine after testing.

The performance of the first P & M road bike was pretty shattering: it could cover the standing quarter mile in 11 seconds, and had a maximum speed approaching 241 kph (150 mph). Despite this performance, it would still average 14–16 k/litre (40–45 mpg) on a run.

Just when P & M had found a winner from a business point of view, disaster struck. One of their employees crashed into a Rover car, writing off the new bike. Fortunately, the rider lived to tell the tale.

Richard Peckett bought the wreck from the insurance company and, using the recoverable parts, built another road machine. Again, it found favour with the motorcycle magazines. This particular machine was soon purchased by a customer, who traded-in his P & M racer in part exchange. As a matter of interest, at the time of writing, the same owner still has the machine and is still using it. After all those years of ownership, the quality and performance speak for themselves.

P & M took another step forward in 1981 when they produced their first monoshock chassis for Jim Wells to race. As usual with a new design, several chassis of this type were sold to customers wishing to have the latest P & M machines.

This was a difficult period for P & M, as the buy-out by Richard Peckett had left him short of development money, and as competitors began to catch up technically, sales began to drop off. Although P & M were unable to introduce completely new innovations every year, they did make continual improvements to their chassis to improve performance. They also tried to make improvements that could be utilized by the owners of older P & M chassis. Considering past customers in this way is a great credit to them. During this period, many customers who sold their P & M racing machines in favour of other makes were disappointed by their new machines, and soon returned to P & M for another chassis that was more to their liking.

In 1983 Richard Peckett designed and built a rising rate rocker arm frame for Jim Wells to race in F1. In addition, P & M built a monoshock frame for F2 racing. This housed a 550 cc Kawasaki,

bored out to 600 cc. Jim Wells also rode this machine.

P & M suffered more interruptions to their normal smooth running in 1984. First they lost their star riders when Jim Wells left with Asa Moyse. They were to ride Harris-made machines in the new F1 750 series. This was a sponsored deal that P & M could not match, and the two riders could not ignore. To add to this, the lease on their factory came to an end and could not be renewed, forcing a move to modern premises, which were purchased.

During 1985, P & M extended their technical expertise even further when they designed a frame that had an adjustable head angle. This could be adjusted from 62 degrees to 64 degrees in $1/2$ degree increments, and the change could be carried out in two or three minutes.

On a competitive machine, this innovation could be a race-winning asset. A test by Alan Cathcart, whose opinion is rated highly, raved about this machine. However, although the 750 cc air-cooled Kawasaki engine produced 101·5 bhp at the rear wheel, this older engine design was no match for the new four-valve Suzuki.

Without the power to win, the new design was destined not to have the opportunity it deserved to prove itself. This is one area where smaller manufacturers lose out on good designs, by not having the resources to develop their innovations.

The following year, 1986, P & M designed and built a monoshock chassis for the new G P Z Kawasaki engine. With this chassis, and an engine

prepared by Mistral Engineering, Ray Swann won the British F2 championship.

By the late 1980s, the sale of new P & M frames had almost ceased. The reduction in demand for special frames is due to the general improvement in factory frames over recent years. This applied to a lesser extent to road machines, but these became one-offs or limited editions, which made manufacture and marketing expensive.

P & M had too much experience not to take advantage of current motorcycle requirements on a commercial basis, and the boom in classic racing provided an outlet for their talents. Having built and raced a Trident, Richard Peckett had invaluable experience in this area, and as the Trident was

very popular with classic racers, P & M soon found a workable business in producing replicas of his original frame.

Richard has two Tridents that he races, while Phil Godfrey has another two, which are raced for him by Phil Davenport, and the business continues to produce these replicas. Although the demand for special racing frames from P & M has almost ceased, the company still holds and maintains all the necessary spares to service the many P & M machines still racing in a variety of club and other events.

From the very beginning, the success of P & M designs speaks for itself, but the build quality matches the design, only the very best materials having been utilized. Frames are manufactured from T45 or Reynolds 531 tubing in 17 and 18 swg. All are nickel-bronze welded. Fork yokes are fabricated steel bronze, welded with different offsets to facilitate the adjustment of trail. These yokes are also produced with standard bores. Head bearings are sealed taper-roller, and to ensure accuracy P & M now finish-bore the head stock after removal from the welding jig. Swinging forks are fabricated from box-section material, with a pressing running down its length to give greater stiffness. Beqarings in swinging rear forks are sealed taper-rollers.

All the P & M frames follow a set specification, this being:

Wheelbase	145–147 cm (57–58 in)
Trail	10–13 cm (4–5 in)
Head Angle	62 degrees
Weight	181 kg (400 lb)
Forks	35 mm Ceriani
Discs	2 × 25 cm (10 in) front; 23 cm (9 in) rear
Calipers/master cylinders Lockheed	
Wheels	CMA five-spoke
Engines	Kawasaki, 100 bhp at rear wheel
	Honda, 105 bhp at rear wheel

Changes to the original specification, in later years, included the use of 38mm Ceriani and Marzocchi forks, Dymag and Astralite wheels, and Spondon discs and four-pot Lockheed calipers. On

Left *A production Trident nearing completion.*

Above left *The man in charge, Richard Peckett.*

Three P & M Tridents wait to do battle. Richard Peckett's works machine is in the foreground.

the design side, the head angle was changed to 63 degrees, while the wheelbase was shortened to 143·5 cm (56$\frac{1}{2}$ in), then 141 cm (55$\frac{1}{2}$ in).

Go it alone?

It is evident that P & M Motorcycles have established a reputation as producers of very competitive and successful racing motorcycle frames. Their results in F1, F2 and endurance racing confirm this. One major factor in this success story is that Richard Peckett also raced the machines he designed and built. This provided essential feedback of the information needed to get the best from a machine.

The handling of P & M machines has always been highly rated, and they have a reputation for being well built. This latter point is borne out by the fact that over 100 frames have been built since the formation of the company in 1975. As far as is known, only one has been destroyed – by a P & M employee who ran into a car on one of the rare occasions when the company produced a road version of their chassis. A large percentage of the others are still putting in racing miles, and are sought after by enthusiasts.

All this sprang from two men who began in a tiny workshop, and extra credit is due when you realize that, in the very beginning, all the tubes used in the frames were bent by hand. This changed, of course,

when the business became established and a purpose-built hydraulic bending machine was finally purchased.

Although P & M's success centred on frame design and construction, it must be mentioned that some of the company's own racing successes were due to the engine building talents of Richard Peckett. He had the ability to squeeze extra performance from factory engines, without sacrificing reliability.

As time passes, trends in motorcycle racing change, the formula formats are revised, and engine sizes altered, while the competitive nature of the sport leads to technical advances. The major factory-produced machines are improved to make the over-the counter racer more competitive, which is one reason why the demand for specially-built frames from the independent manufacturers has dropped off. Although there will always be independent chassis manufacturers and a market for their products, it would appear that they have to be more specialized. P & M have recognized this, and have responded to the commercial needs of business by exploiting the now-popular classic bike racing.

From 1975 to the time of writing, the range of machines produced by P & M has enjoyed a very good following. It is interesting to speculate on what the company may produce in the future. Perhaps a new racing formula will open the door again, or possibly P & M may accept the expense and administration requirements of marketing a road machine. Whatever they choose to design and manufacture, motorcycling enthusiasts will benefit from machines admired by many.

10

▰▰▰▰▰ PDQ

Not all the people with the ability to build motor-cycle frames actually turn their skills into a big business. However, one person who has made a significant contribution to frame-making technology, while continuing to run a normal motorcycle sales and preparation business, is Larry Webb, the proprietor of P D Q.

Larry began his association with motorcycles by working in various retailers' workshops, where valuable mechanical experience was gained. As his knowledge grew, so did the desire to do this type of work for himself, in his own business. During 1977, while working for Motor Racing Enterprises on racing cars, he finally decided to make the break and work for himself. His late employers rented him a workshop at the rear of their premises, and Larry was in business.

The first title Larry used for his enterprise was L D M. This new business catered for those who required machines prepared for racing, or who wanted modifications to frames. In most cases, these modifications were, hardly surprisingly, to improve the structural performance of machines being used in competition.

Spending time on race frame modification led eventually to the design and construction of the first complete motorcycle frame. This was built from round-section steel tubing, and was designed to accommodate an H 2 R Kawasaki 750 cc engine.

The completed machine was notable in one respect, and that was its size. Although the frame held a 750 cc engine, the machine's overall size was similar to that of a 250 cc racer. Larry claims that this frame was the first ever to boast fully-floating

rear suspension, which he conceived to solve a problem half-way through construction, rather than it being an integral part of the design from the beginning.

Larry built the machine as a one-off, for his personal use, and raced it in U K clubman events for two seasons. No great results are reported, but he says that his novice status as a rider may have been a contributory factor.

During this period, the main income for L D M still came from modification work and rebuilds. Then an opportunity arose for him to go back to working on race cars, for Johnny Dumfries, which was too tempting to pass up. As a result L D M ceased trading. However, Larry did not forget single-cylinder engines, as he spent some time working on go-karts. Then he received, and accepted, an offer to work for Eddy Kidd, the world-famous stunt rider. This meant working on motorcycle frames again.

Larry was required to strengthen frames to cope with the landing loads from the record-breaking jumps made by Eddy Kidd. This was in addition to

the general preparation and maintenance of all the machines used in the stunts. At the end of a two-year stint, however, it was back to working on cars again. Then the firm that employed him folded, so he decided to go into business again.

P D Q was formed in 1984 as a general motorcycle workshop, catering for rebuilds, modifications, and the retail of motorcycles, spares and accessories. However, Larry Webb was to become involved in the construction of another interesting design. During the late 1980s, in conjunction with Norman Hossack, he built a machine that had a unique front suspension layout.

The Norman Hossack design was for a wishbone-type front suspension. This was based on rigid, rectangular-section steel vertical members which, in effect, replaced the normal fork legs. These were mounted to the frame by means of a pair of wishbones, the lower one operating the cantilever-mounted single damper unit. Steering was taken care of by rotation of the whole upright in a bearing head that replaced the original head.

In order to develop this suspension, the front

Below left Larry Webb aboard the first machine designed and built by himself.

Below A pair of stunt bikes strengthened and prepared by Larry Webb for Eddy Kidd.

was removed from Larry Webb's Kawasaki GPZ1100B1 frame, and the new front welded on. The rear suspension utilized the original Kawasaki rear fork with additional bracing welded on to enhance stiffness.

This design of front suspension was claimed to be more rigid, while the steering geometry remained more constant during braking and cornering. It was also claimed as an added bonus to have improved suspension response.

At the time Larry Webb carried out this conversion to his personal Kawasaki, it was agreed that PDQ would perfect the system for road use and convert customers' machines, while Norman Hossack would cater for the race versions. However, for the usual commercial reasons, PDQ did not pursue the project.

Norman Hossack continued to carry out this conversion for both road and race use, and to date various large-engined Japanese machines have received the treatment, along with a few BMWs and a Laverda. PDQ meanwhile, made a wide variety of modifications to road machines, one of which has become popular. It is the conversion of the Yamaha V-Max to single-leg rear suspension, while retaining its shaft drive.

During 1990, PDQ built another rather special frame. This housed a Suzuki GT750 engine, the machine being designed for drag racing. It was an interesting project, as the lower frame tubes from the original factory frame had to be retained. This was to comply with the relevant class regulations.

The frame was based on a large, deep-section spine, which was fabricated from steel. The

remainder of the frame was constructed from round steel tubing, and included the obligatory tubes from the original frame. Suitable front forks and swinging rear fork completed this special-purpose frame. The unique design was successful in taking several wins in its class.

Suspension and suspense

Although PDQ may not have been prolific frame makers to date, Larry Webb's claim to be the first to produce the fully-floating rear suspension, his involvement in the wishbone front suspension, and his endless frame modifications, are all contributions to the advancement of motorcycle frame technology. With such proven ability, who knows what PDQ might be involved with in the future.

Opposite *The Yamaha V-Max converted by PDQ to single-leg rear suspension, while retaining the shaft drive. This is a standard conversion offered by the company.*

Above *This frame was built by PDQ to compete in drag racing. It makes use of a large-section spine, but retains the down tubes of the original bike to comply with the relevant class regulations.*

CHAPTER

11

▮▮▮▮▮▮ Quasar

A motorcycle that the rider sits in, rather than on, with feet forward, and under a roof, must be considered unique. The Quasar was just such a design.

Quasar was the brainchild of Malcolm Newell, a keen English motorcyclist. 'Keen' is almost an understatement, as Malcolm has owned over 140 motorcycles. He began his commercial career in motorcycling by managing a motorcycle shop, which eventually led to him running his own shop.

Even though the shop was his own business, Malcolm eventually decided that retailing was not as rewarding as construction, so the shop was replaced with a workshop. This decision was taken during the 1960s and early 1970s, and led to a few one-off bikes and trikes being designed and built. During the course of this work, Malcolm met Ken Leaman, an engineer who agreed with him that the idea of a motorcycle that was sat in, rather than on, appeared to offer many advantages. These included a lower centre of gravity and improved aerodynamics. The result of their collaboration was to become Quasar.

Without sufficient capital and engineering facilities, they handed over the project to a company called Wilson and Sons, in 1972. That company produced the first pre-production machines, followed by ten production models. Wilson and Sons then handed the Quasar project to another company, which became known as Quasar Motorcycles Ltd. This new company produced another ten examples, but unfortunately ceased to trade immediately afterwards. While all this was going on, Malcolm Newell had set about producing a hub-centre steering system, based on a Bob Tait patent.

To raise the capital to finance the hub-centre steering project. Malcolm produced some machines called Phasars, which were basically standard machines that incorporated a twin-head steering system. A total of 20 machines with this unique twin-head system was produced. By 1984, Malcolm was again concentrating on the design and construction of Quasars, resulting in the Mk II.

The Mk I Quasar, built by the two previously-mentioned companies, had a tubular-steel frame, which housed an in-line, four-cylinder, 850 cc Reliant engine. It retained the Reliant four-speed gearbox, which had synchromesh on all gears and shaft-drive to the rear wheel. The front suspension and steering were by a leading-link system, while the rear featured a swinging arm.

The bodywork was of fibreglass and incorporated a windscreen and full roof. This arrangement offered improved aerodynamics over a conventional motorcycle, and gave the rider much better weather protection. The pillion passenger also shared the same creature comforts.

The machine's long wheelbase (200·7 cm/79 in), coupled with the low riding position, resulted in excellent stability, especially during cornering. As a result, Quasar offered both performance and comfort.

The Mk II differed from the Mk I in several ways, there being significant technical changes. Although the frame was of similar layout and retained the sit-in/feet-forward riding position, it employed hub-centre steering, while the choice of engine and its position differed. High-performance, Japanese, multi-cylinder, across-the-frame engines were utilized. Moreover, a major design change moved the engine's position from in front of the rider, to behind the rider.

The Mk II Quasar, with an even lower centre of gravity, and the suspension advantages associated with hub-centre steering, produced exciting performance and handling potential. This was complemented by very-low-drag bodywork that was roofless. The result was a machine that offered very high speed with handling to match.

When in production, the Mk II Quasar could be purchased in kit form, and was not restricted to any specific engine. Over ten of these Mk II versions were sold.

In 1992 Malcolm Newell designed his latest creation. Although he refers to it as Quasar Mk III, it is an entirely new invention and, therefore, is a concept vehicle. Vehicle is a safe description, as it can have three or more wheels.

Engine, transmission, five-gallon tank, battery and exhaust system all at or below wheel spindle height. (EMAP)

Quasar Mk III is a banking vehicle, in which each pair of wheels (on the same axle line) is interconnected by means of a mechanical rocking arm, or a hydraulic, electrical or pneumatic equivalent. This arrangement enables the interconnected wheels to maintain a relatively equal contact pressure with the ground while the vehicle banks. The rocking arm, or equivalent, may be locked in any position by means of a disc brake and caliper (or other system), which prevents the vehicle from banking and can hold it in a vertical position without the operator having to balance it. The rocking arm, or its equivalent, always remains parallel to the ground. This enables the fitting of aerodynamic control surfaces, which remain parallel to the ground while the vehicle banks.

In today's increasingly heavy traffic, the motorcycle provides the most time- and space-effective means of transporting one or two people. However, where safety and comfort are concerned, it is greatly inferior to the car. To provide adequate levels of safety, the occupants of cars must be restrained within a rigid shell, capable of withstanding a major impact. It is not possible to provide this with a conventional motorcycle. Malcolm Newell's invention makes it possible to produce a narrow-tracked vehicle in which the occupants are fully enclosed by a rigid shell that does not have to be balanced while stationary.

The method of interlinking the wheels in the basic design can be achieved in a number of ways.

In one case, a leaf spring provides both the interlinking connection and shock absorption; in another, the interlinking rocker arm is connected to dampers with coil springs. The latter arrangement allows the suspension and rocker arm to be replaced by electrical, hydraulic or pneumatic linkages.

In each case, as the vehicle banks, all wheels remain in contact with the ground; this is ensured by a centrally-mounted pivot for the rocking arm, leaf spring, etc. The mechanism of support provides a parallelogram of linkages. The upper and lower swinging arms are pivoted from four points attached to either the front or rear bulkhead, or both. The arms extend backwards, or forwards, of the pivot points, and connect with the two kingpin posts. The arms are free to rotate only in a vertical plane. Thus, one wheel is free to move in a vertical plane, independently of the other, but within the constraint of the available suspension movement.

At the time of writing, no machine is available to give an indication of the potential of this exciting new invention, or what the public reaction to a completely new concept of this type might be. As revolutionary as Quasar was when first introduced, Malcolm Newell made it work and work well. Although in comparatively small numbers, it was produced and sold. This totally new vehicle should excite a number of potential customers, and a definite development programme is planned. Perhaps, by the time this book is published, the machine will be in full production.

Laid back

New motorcycle designs are always welcome, and Malcolm Newell has certainly provided his fair share. His latest brainchild may yet gain him world recognition and the reward that goes with it, but from a brilliant idea to a marketable product is a giant step. Only time will tell if Malcolm manages to take that step.

The Quasar presented at the 1975 Earls Court Show was welded in Reynolds 531 tubing, the frame had rectangular section pivoted forks at both ends with Girling gas-fillled struts. As Vic Willoughby pointed out in the Motor Cycle, 'Ticking over in Malcolm Newell's mind are thoughts of hub centre steering'. (EMAP)

∎∎∎∎∎∎ Rickman

During the 1960s and 1970s, the name Rickman needed no introduction to European motorcycling enthusiasts. Their high reputation began with the design and production of motocross frames, although at that time the sport was known as scrambling. Road racing frames followed, as did road-legal motorcycles.

The company was formed by two brothers, Derek and Don Rickman, both of whom had been successful scrambles riders. Derek began competing on BSA machines during 1950, while Don followed two years later, also on a BSA. Their competition careers were to prove invaluable when they began to build scrambles frames, as they had first-hand knowledge of what was required from that type of machine. Moreover, they had gained many contacts in the motorcycle industry. These contacts led to them deciding to go into the motorcycle trade.

In 1958 the Rickman brothers opened a retail motorcycle shop in New Milton, in the south of England. By that time, they had also decided that they wanted to build their own scramblers, or motocross, machines. With the help of Tiny Camfield, of road racing fame, they began to build a machine for Derek. This first Rickman machine consisted of a Triumph T100 mounted in a modified BSA frame, with a BSA gearbox and Norton forks. A similar machine was built for Don.

Above *The production Rickman Bultaco Metisse.*

Left *Derek Rickman scrambling a Metisse Mk III fitted with a Matchless engine.*

Right *To prove that both Rickman brothers were serious competitors, here is Don aboard a Metisse powered by a Bultaco engine.*

Metisse was the name given to the Rickman machines from the very beginning, and it continued to be used until the company stopped building bikes. There is an interesting story behind the use of this name. The first Rickman machine was built using major components from several different factory machines and, therefore, was very much a hybrid. Since the French for hybrid, 'metisse', sounded right, it was chosen as the name that would be applied to all Rickman frames.

During 1960, the Mk II Metisse was produced. Again, this utilized a modified BSA frame, but it differed from the Mk I in that the incorporation of fibreglass components led to significant improvements. Doug Mitchenal, of Avon Fairings, had put forward the idea that fibreglass could be used to great advantage, and the result was that the Mk II Metisse sported a combined seat and tail unit, which incorporated the air filter, oil tank, and plates

Left One of three identical motocross machines campaigned by the Rickman brothers and Eddie Burroughs. The engine is the G85 C S 500 cc Matchless. These machines were built with future production in mind; note the distinctive fibreglass panels.

Below The engine mounting details of a Mk III Metisse frame, built for a Triumph engine with separate gearbox. Note the cutaway to show the filter arrangement.

Above *This late 1960s photograph shows the Mk IV Metisse frame. It differed from the previous model by having head and down tubes with a greater sweep back. The engine is a B S A B40 Victor.*

Below *It is not surprising that motocross machines were an important part of the company's work, given that both of the Rickman brothers were competitors.*

Left A Metisse road racing frame for a non-unit Triumph twin. In the finished machine, the engine was faired in.

Below left An example of the first road racing frame designed and built by Rickman. This early version could accommodate the Matchless G45 or G50 engine. In the hands of Bill Ivy, the prototype won its very first race at a British National Championship meeting during 1966.

Below right The C R (Café Racer) Metisse, a road-going version of the race frame. This example has a Triumph engine and was supplied to the famous Giacomo Agostini.

for the competition numbers. This unit was actually bonded to the BSA frame. At the time, this was quite innovative and bound to attract attention.

The first Rickman-designed and built frame appeared in 1961, and it became the Metisse Mk III. It was constructed from 1¼in diameter Reynolds 531 tubing with a 16 swg wall thickness. Ken Sprayson, technical engineer of the Reynolds Tube Company, was of considerable assistance during the development of this frame, as was the Siff Bronze Company, who gave invaluable help with the bronze welding technique used. This excellent form of welding was utilized on all subsequent Rickman frames. Such attention to detail and quality was to become a feature of Rickman products.

A prototype batch of three identical Mk III Metisse frames was built to house 500 cc Matchless engines. The fibreglass parts were all finished in the very distinctive British Racing Green.

At this time, the frames were being built purely for the personal use of the Rickman brothers, the extra machine being for Eddie Burroughs, who had joined the business. However, they were also built with future production in mind, which was one of the reasons for the use of the Matchless engine. Matchless were prepared to supply Rickman with engine and gearbox units directly from the factory, whereas Triumph factory were not.

In many ways, the Matchless engine was ideal, particularly for scrambling. It was strong, tunable, and comparatively easy to maintain. Therefore, it turned out to be a very wise choice for the Metisse.

The Rickman brothers, being very accomplished scramble riders, were the ideal marketing tool for the new machine. Their successes soon drew attention to the Metisse, which led to requests for replica kits. In a very short time, orders began to flood in, not only from the UK, but also from Europe and, a little later, from America and Australia.

The Mk III frame was soon adapted to accept the Triumph engine, and over the next few years the Metisse became one of the most popular scrambles machines available. An example of this popularity was that at the 1964 Moto Cross de Nations, at Hawkstone, over half the riders were mounted on Metisse motorcycles.

During this early successful period for the Metisse in motocross, many famous riders were to take advantage of the Rickman frame. These included Nic Jansen and Hubert Scaillet from Belgium, Andy Lee and Ivor England from England, and Sten Lundin from Sweden. Film stars Steve McQueen and Clint Walker, from the USA, were also Metisse fans. The business potential from the USA was sufficient for an agent to be appointed, which resulted in many frame kits being sold there.

During 1964, production of the Metisse frames had outgrown the workshop at the back of the Rickmans' retail shop, and as the future looked excellent, new factory premises were acquired in New Milton. More staff were employed, some of whom were also competitive riders. This speaks highly of the esteem in which the Rickman name was held. It was at this time that Herbert Evemy (a school friend) joined the company as a director.

During the latter part of 1965, a prototype Mk IV Metisse was built. This model had a different frame layout, the head and down tubes being swept back more. The new frame was originally built to accommodate the Triumph T100 engine, which was of unit construction, the engine and gearbox being one

assembly. Later, the BSA B40 Victor engine was also utilized. In addition to the new frame layout, all the fibreglass panels were redesigned, the styling being sharpened to create a new look.

Earlier, in 1963, the Rickman brothers had gone to Spain to develop a motocross machine for the Bultaco factory. When they returned, they brought with them a 200 cc Bultaco engine. This was fitted into a much-modified Mk III Metisse frame. One major modification to the frame was that it had a single front down tube in place of the normal twin down tubes. This machine was known as the Petite Metisse, and it was the first two-stroke-engined machine ever built by Rickman.

The two-stroke Metisse proved popular, and a few years later, when Bultaco produced a 250 cc engine, Rickman designed a completely new frame to accommodate the new engine. Modified versions of the Mk IV fibreglass panels were used. This particular model was the first complete motorcycle that the Rickman brothers offered on the UK market, and over 500 were sold. Bultaco produced an identical model, which was sold world wide, although mainly in the USA.

A dramatic change was to occur at Rickman in

Above *CR 750 four cylinder.*

Above left *An early Triumph-engined CR Metisse. Note the disc brake, a very advanced feature for the 1960s.*

Left *A later version of the Triumph CR Metisse.*

1966. Until then, their designs were mainly for motocross and some street-legal machines. However, an approach was made by Tim Kirby and BP's racing manager, who asked Rickman to look at the possibility of designing and building a road racing frame.

Rickman rose to the occasion, producing a road race frame that was an immediate success in every sense of the word. Ridden by Bill Ivy, it won first

time out at a British National Championship meeting at Mallory Park. This first model could accommodate Matchless G45 and G50 engines.

Success in road racing led to a demand for replicas of the Rickman frame, so it was put into full production. The frame was built to house a variety of engines, including Matchless G45 and G50, Triumph 500 and 650 cc and Norton 750 cc. A modified version of this frame was built to house

an Italian Aermacchi engine, while other engines used were the Weslake road racing engine and, a few years later, the Helmut Fath four-cylinder engine. One interesting point about the road racing frame is that it was tilted with one of the first disc brakes used on a motorcycle.

The success of the Rickman frame caught the attention of a British police force, for whom the company built a model based on a slightly modified road race frame. This housed a Triumph engine and was fitted with fibreglass bodywork tailored specifically for police use.

Rickman modified the police type frame and used it to produce a street-legal motorcycle. Initially, it was fitted with the Triumph engine, but later in 1974, was altered so that the four-cylinder Honda, Suzuki and Kawasaki engines could be fitted. This model was designated C R, short for café racer. Later, the frame received further slight modifications. It was fitted with a one-piece fairing and body unit, the result being the Rickman Endurance.

All of these new models sold in considerable numbers. Fortunately, Rickman were quite capable of coping with volume production, having made yet another move to a much larger factory in 1969. This move had been made to allow production of 125 and 250 cc machines for the American market.

The 125 cc machine utilized a Zundapp engine and was produced as both a motocross version and a s treet-legal Enduro. The 250 cc machine used a Montessa engine and was built in motocross form only. Production of these machines rose to 72 machines per week, and over a three-year period many thousands were shipped to the U S A.

The Zundapp-engined Enduro model was developed for rural police use, being sold to forces throughout the U K during the early 1970s. Later, a similar model was developed for the S A S.

One famous rider to start his career on a Rickman Zundapp 125 was Graham Noyce, who rode one in schoolboy events. Later, he joined Rickman as an apprentice toolmaker, but went on to ride the factory 125 and 250 cc machines. During 1973, a special-framed 400 cc Husky was built for Graham, on which he won many races before he was signed up for the Maico factory.

Another commercial venture for Rickman during the early 1970s came about when 130 Royal Enfield

engines were offered to the factory. Once again, the ever-faithful, street-legal Metisse frame was called upon, being modified to accept the Enfield engine. The result was a batch of complete road-going machines.

During the 1970s, Rickman were to experience at first hand the effect of the stranglehold the Japanese were beginning to gain on the market. Japanese competition machines were cheaper, due to the huge backing of the factories. This led to rapid development, which soon began to eclipse the more expensive Rickman models. Unfortunately, much the same happened to the road-going machines. It is said that the early Japanese street machines had poor handling, but they were powered by superb engines. Again, with their immense resources, the Japanese soon began to produce frames to match the engines, and this left little room in the market for the Rickman frames. One wonders if any Rickman creations – or for that matter Harris, or Bakker, or any of the other machines featured in this book, were ever stripped down under an appraising oriental eye…

As a result of the diminishing market, 1980 saw the Rickman brothers reluctantly give up the design

Above *Rickman found a big market in the U S A for small-capacity motocross machines. Here a Metisse frame houses a 125 cc Zundapp engine.*

Opposite *A version of the Zundapp-engined Metisse built for the British S A S.*

and manufacture of motorcycle frames. However, the Rickman name continued and, at the time of writing, is still linked to the production of motorcycle accessories, such as fairings, safety bars, carriers, and a range of luggage and helmet boxes. Ironically, these are made to fit most current Japanese models.

Distinguished service

Although no longer independent frame makers, the Rickman brothers made a significant contribution to the development of motorcycle frames, having dominated the motocross market, and then produced successful road racing frames and street-legal machines. No book on independent motorcycle frame makers would be complete without a record of their contribution.

13

▌▌▌▌▌ Colin Seeley Racing

The name Colin Seeley needs no introduction in the world of motorcycling. Long before he became renowned for the design and manufacture of racing motorcycles, he had enjoyed a very successful career as a racing sidecar rider.

During 1960 Colin was riding solo scramble machines and began to race sidecar outfits in road racing. Towards the end of that year, he bought a G50 Matchless and modified it to accept a sidecar. With this machine his sidecar career got under way.

Success with the Seeley-modified Matchless was immediate. During that first season, he earned his international licence, and in his first ever Isle of Man TT, he finished in a splendid sixth position. By 1962 his performances were becoming more and more consistent. In fact, he became British Champion that year. Riding his sidecar outfit, he was the highest-placed British rider in the major interna-

tional events. He took the British Championship again in 1964. This success as a racing sidecar rider resulted in Colin Seeley being placed third in the 1964 World Championships, a place he also gained in 1966.

All this competitive motorcycling was in addition to running a business, which he began at a very early age. After leaving school, Colin had begun an engineering apprenticeship, but his dynamism soon led him to drop this, and shortly after he set up his own business. This was a retail motorcycle shop. An amazing fact is that at the time he was only 18 years old. At a later stage, the business was to become an AMC agent, and this led to his close association with the AJS 7R and the Matchless G50 machines.

Although it might appear that Colin Seeley had his plate full with running his business and a full

Above *The Mk1 Seeley, with a Matchless G50 engine. The machine appeared in 1965 and was to set Colin on the road to becoming an independent manufacturer.*

Right *Colin Seeley's interest in motorcycles stemmed from an early age. Here, at 14, he gets the feel of his father's Vincent.*

Left *Sidecar racing was to prove a successful venture for Colin, shown here during the Dutch TT in 1964, the year he came third in the world championship. The outfit is powered by a Rennsport BMW.*

sidecar racing programme, he still found time to build a solo racing frame. AMC ceased production of the 7Rs and G50s in the 1960s, but Colin felt that both engines still had something to offer, so he decided to build a frame to house the 500 cc G50 Matchless engine. Many parts for the original machine were no longer available, and Colin considered the original frames to be too heavy and complicated, so he set out to manufacture a frame of his own design.

The first frame was built completely by hand,

Left *The handmade Mk1 frame gave a new lease of life to both the Matchless G50 and the AJS 7R engines.*

Right *Derek Minter at speed on the Mk1.*

Below *Colin (left) discusses the merits of the Mk1 Seeley with Derek Minter, who was to ride the machine on its successful debut, winning first time out.*

Below right *Colin proudly displays the Mk2 Seeley prototype during the Isle of Man TT in 1967; a Mk1 is in the background. The latest frame offered a considerable saving in weight without any loss of structural integrity.*

Below The Mk3 Seeley displayed a complete change in frame layout. Diagonal tubes ran from the steering head down to the rear swinging arm pivot, the engine being suspended below them for improved accessibility.

Left The great Mike Hailwood demonstrates the potential of the Seeley Mk3.

Right Colin refined the Seeley in 1970, producing the M4 version. This is the works 636 version.

using a simple manual pipe bender to shape the frame tubes. These were made from 3cm (1¼in) diameter 16 swg Reynolds 531 steel tubing, filled with silver sand during bending to prevent distortion. No jigs were used in the assembly. The whole frame was built on a metal-topped bench, or surface table, working from a marked centre-line and with a threaded tool that could be adjusted to support the steering head at the required angles. The tubes were carefully fitted together and then welded by Colin, a self-taught welder. This Mk1 frame was fitted with a Matchless G500 engine, and the first Seeley Racing solo motorcycle was born. The year was 1965.

At the start of the 1966 season, Derek Minter rode Seeley machines, and what a start it was. He won first time out on both a 350 cc (7R) version and a 500 cc (G50) model. A new era of frame building was on the way; at the time there were few independent frame makers to carry out this type of design and manufacture.

That year also saw the AMC factory go into receivership, and Colin Seeley bought the whole racing department, that is the remainder of the spares and the rights to carry on production of the 7R and G50 engines. Included in the deal were the rights to the Manx Norton, which had previously been taken over by AMC. He continued to supply Manx spares from the residual stock, and manufactured some, such as cam pushers, while there was a demand.

All this was a very bold step. Colin Seeley was about to undertake the manufacture of racing frames to house engines that had been dropped some years earlier by the original manufacturers.

History, however, shows that the decision gave the racing motorcycle world new and competitive machines.

John Blanchard had taken over from Derek Minter as Seeley's rider during 1966, and continued into 1967. Success on the Seeley G50 was topped in that year when Blanchard took fourth place in the Isle of Man Senior TT. After this, however, a disagreement resulted in John Blanchard opting not to ride for Seeley, the talented John Cooper taking over for the remainder of 1967.

In his usual quest to advance, Colin Seeley produced the Mk2 machine for the 1968 season. Although the Mk1 had proved both popular with its riders and successful, Colin felt that it was too heavy. The new frame still remained a full-loop type of very similar layout to the Mk1, but the Reynolds 531 frame tubes were of smaller diameter at 1⅛in, while the tube wall thickness was reduced to 17 swg. These changes resulted in a considerable reduction in weight, without any reduction in structural performance.

Dave Croxford was to ride the new Seeley during the 1968 season. Again, the machine enjoyed many successes, as well as many notable battles with the Rickman Metisse, but the culmination of the season saw Dave Croxford winning the 1968 British Championship.

By this time, not only was the Seeley a very successful design, but the motorcycle fraternity had also taken to it, and its popularity continued to grow. In the meantime, Seeley continued to service existing AMC customers from the stock of original spares and parts manufactured by Colin Seeley Racing Developments Ltd.

Experience gained during a race season gives a designer the information required to ensure that his machine remains competitive, and Colin Seeley has always been a man to make the most of that experience. This was what led to the Seeley Mk3.

Produced during 1969 and 1970, the Mk3 still utilized the proven Reynolds 531 steel tubing for its frame, but the frame layout changed. It was no longer a full-loop type; there were no down tubes, and to produce the required structural performance, diagonal tubes ran from the steering head to the swinging rear fork pivot. Colin had established that the fixing of these two points in relation to each

other was a major factor in producing a stiff frame which, in turn, improved stability on the track or the road.

Another significant improvement was engine access. The diagonal frame layout meant that the engine was suspended below the main tubes, leaving it exposed for work in situ, or making total removal much easier and quicker than with the full-loop Mk1 and Mk2.

During 1969 Vincent Davey sponsored Mick Andrews, Dave Potter and Dave Croxford to ride Seeley 7R and G50 engined machines. A successful season for this sponsor was topped when Dave

Croxford won the British 500 cc Championship. The Mk 3 frame was an immediate success, showing that Colin Seeley Racing was continuing to develop frame technology to remain competitive on the track and in the commercial world.

The Mk 3 continued into 1970, but towards the end of that year, Colin Seeley produced yet another frame advance, the Mk 4. Although the Mk 3 had been successful, there was room for improvement, and Seeley was not slow to recognize the fact.

The significant differences on the Mk 4 were the long diagonal tubes running up from the swinging rear fork pivot to the bottom of the steering head,

Above left *The Mk 4 continued in production until 1973, and this 1972 version is typical of the breed.*

Left *In 1967 a Seeley frame was built to house the U R S four-cylinder 500, an engine originally developed by Helmut Fath for sidecar racing.*

Below *The across-the-frame engine layout of the URS can be clearly seen in this shot, as can the details of the Seeley frame.*

and the seat tubes, which were joined to the top of the steering head. This arrangement was the reverse of the tube positions in the previous designs.

The change resulted in a better structural position for the main down-tubes. The Mk 4 can be identified by the fact that these tubes are lower at the head end and, with A M C engines, run on each side of the engine rather than over it. Engine access was still excellent. The Mk 4 frame was produced until Colin Seeley Racing ceased production of motorcycles in late 1973.

Throughout production of the Seeley frames, Colin made full use of the 350 cc 7R and the 500 cc G50 engines, but these were far from being exclusive choices. Colin also designed and built many frames to house a wide range of engine makes and forms. Some became series-production frames, being produced in considerable numbers.

One of the first deviations from the use of A M C engines occurred during 1967, when a frame was designed and built to house an in-line, four-cylinder 500 cc U R S engine. This had been developed originally by Helmut Fath and raced in sidecars. The performance of this engine had already been

Above left The Mk3 frame provided the basis for the Kuhn Seeley Norton. Powered by the Norton Commando twin, the machine was assembled and sold by Kuhn Motors, using frame kits supplied by Seeley.

Left The remarkable Barry Sheene, in his early days, aboard a Kuhn Seeley Commando.

Above Alan Barnett and Colin Seeley with the Q U B 500 at Brands Hatch during 1970.

Right Piloted by Alan Barnett, the Q U B 500 is put through its paces at Brands. Sadly, the engine proved troublesome and development was halted.

Left John Cooper aboard the Yamsel prototype. Unlike *QUB*, this machine was to prove successful.

Below left In 1971 Seeley introduced the G50-engined Condor road bike, shown here being tested by motorcycle journalist Mick Woollett.

Above The Italian company Ducati recognized Seeley's skills when they commissioned Colin to build a series of frames for their 500 cc V-twin. These were ridden by Paul Smart and Bruno Spaggiari.

proven, having won Fath two world sidecar titles.

Colin Seeley's frame did justice to the URS engine, the machine taking John Blanchard to a superb fourth place in the Ulster Grand Prix. Unfortunately, just after this important victory, Blanchard and Seeley parted company, so the potential of this rider and machine combination was never fully explored.

In 1969 Colin Seeley housed yet another type of engine in one of his frames. In this case, the frame was a Mk3, and the engine was the twin-cylinder Norton Commando. This Norton-engined machine was developed for Kuhn Motors, who marketed it. Once the machine had been developed, Seeley continued to supply frame kits, while Kuhn Motors completed the build and sold them on.

In 1970 Colin Seeley designed and built a frame to house a two-stroke engine, the 500 cc QUB. This interesting project was a joint venture between Queens University, Belfast and Seeley. The engine was designed at the university, while Colin Seeley was not only involved in its manufacture, but also built the remainder of the bike. Although it showed performance potential, it was troublesome, and the project died for various reasons before the problems could be overcome.

Another engine make was to receive the Seeley treatment during this period. It was a Husqvarna 500 cc air-cooled twin. That year also saw the introduction of the successful Yamsel prototype, ridden by John Cooper.

In the following year, Colin Seeley utilized his frame-making skills to house a variety of engine makes and types, and also built the first frames for Boyer Racing. One very significant point about 1971 was that a G50 engine and Seeley frame combination was produced as a road bike. This road-going Seeley was named the Condor, a small production batch being completed and sold.

During 1970–1 Seeley was contracted by the Italian Ducati factory to produce a series of frames for their works 500 cc V-twin. Paul Smart and Bruno Spaggiari were the riders. Two much-admired examples of these frames still live in the UK. They were raced successfully with 750 cc versions of the V-twin engine.

Another marked indication of the regard being shown for Colin Seeley's work came in 1971, when the legendary Barry Sheene, then a Suzuki works rider, suggested that they should consider a Seeley frame to replace the works frame of the X R O 5, a 500 cc, air-cooled two-stroke twin. (Sorry to use the word 'legendary', but what would you say?) The Suzuki riders were experiencing handling problems with this machine, hence the approach to Seeley. The resultant Seeley-framed version was ridden to an excellent third place in the 1971 Senior T T.

Barry Sheene then took this machine to Mallory Park and finished second to Giacomo Agostini on the 500 cc M V Augusta, on which he had just won the Senior T T. In 1973 Sheene won both the British 500 Championship and the European 750 Championship on the Suzuki-Seeley, then powered by a water-cooled, three-cylinder engine. This convinced Suzuki U K that Colin Seeley was the man to build their future chassis.

Great success during this period of the Seeley Suzuki combination resulted in Colin receiving one of their newly-imported T R 500 11 engines to utilize in another of his advanced projects during 1973. At the time, he was not only running Colin Seeley Racing Developments Ltd, but also overseeing the production of Brabham racing cars, which were in

the transition from tubular space-frame chassis to monocoque construction. Seeing this development taking place in racing cars, he decided that motorcycles could also take advantage of this technology. The Suzuki TR50011 found its way into the first Seeley monocoque motorcycle.

Left Colin Seeley's involvement with Brabham racing cars led to the development of a monocoque motorcycle frame. Powered by a Suzuki TR500 engine, it is shown here being tried for size by Ian Simpson, while Ron Carnell, competition manager for Duckhams, looks on.

Below left A variety of engines have found their way into Seeley frames over the years, including this 750cc Weslake parallel twin.

Below The Seeley Honda was an impressive and successful machine. It led to further contracts from the Japanese manufacturer to produce special machines.

The box-like monocoque construction was fabricated from aluminium sheet and riveted together. It had many advantages over a steel tubing frame construction. Sheet being formed and riveted did not suffer from the distortion problems common to welded frames, while the large-section box structure led to greater stiffness. Moreover, this type of construction offered ease of production.

The first example of the Seeley monocoque also utilized Colin Seeley's own custom-built magnesium alloy wheels and other specialized parts. At the time, it looked like the way forward for motorcycle chassis technology.

Although the machine was ridden with great promise by Barry Sheene, this interesting development came too close to the time when Colin Seeley Racing ceased trading. As a result, the potential of this very interesting project was never fulfilled.

Prior to the monocoque development, Colin Seeley was still busy building tubular frames for a

variety of engines. In 1972 a Weslake 750 cc parallel twin was fitted to a Seeley frame, then in 1973 two other interesting powerplants were to be accommodated. One was a 750 cc two-stroke from Kawasaki, and the other a 750 cc water-cooled triple from Suzuki.

Although 1973 had seen some interesting engines given the Seeley treatment, in most cases these were one-offs. With the 7R and G50 engines having reached the end of their competitive careers, and faced by the difficulties of maintaining a factory and a staff of almost 30 people in a declining market for racing or race-bred motorcycles, Colin Seeley ceased trading. However, his skills and experience were not to rest too long, as in 1975 Seeley International was formed.

Close contact with Honda UK resulted in the Seeley-Honda. This bike comprised the Japanese company's SOHC, air-cooled four-cylinder engine in a Seeley frame.

It was such an impressive and successful machine that Honda UK contracted Colin Seeley to produce a batch of 150 road-going replicas of Phil Read's 1977 TT-winning machine. This was more of a conversion than a scratch-build and required the fitting of race-type fairings and ancillary equipment to an existing machine. So successful was this project that Honda pretty soon engaged Seeley International on another contract.

Seeley had already built trials frames for the TL200 four-stroke engine, which had been ridden by Honda works riders. This resulted in a plan for Seeley International to produce 1000 production models. Unfortunately, after building just 300 TL200s, the company suffered considerable financial losses, so 1980 saw Seeley International cease trading as a motorcycle manufacturer in any form. However, Colin Seeley remained in business in other areas.

Original replicas

Although Colin Seeley's skill, flair and finesse are no longer being utilized in the design and construction of high-performance motorcycles, he has left his mark quite clearly in this area. As this account shows, he has built a wide range of machines for a wide range of engines. Many of these machines were ridden with great success in competition. In fact, to this day, Seeley machines are still raced in classic events.

Throughout the period when Seeley machines were produced, they enjoyed a reputation for being well built, very neat and having an excellent finish. The high standard of construction is borne out by the large number that are still in existence. Seeley machines are very much sought after by collectors and riders.

The esteem in which these classic Seeley machines are held is reflected in the high prices they make on the rare occasions when original examples become available. In some cases, prices are even higher than those commanded by the factory-made machines using the same engines.

Although some Seeley machines were made in considerable numbers, the demand for these classics far outweighs the supply of genuine examples.

Above *The TL200 Honda-based trials bike proved a successful machine, but caused financial problems, leading to Seeley International being wound up.*

Left *The design of the Seeley Honda frame allowed removal of the cylinder head while the engine was still in the bike, something that was not possible on the standard machine.*

This has resulted in replicas being produced. In fact, other frame makers have made a business of producing these copies. In most cases, they are marketed as replicas, and not sold as originals. Again, this emphasizes the respect and interest that motorcycling enthusiasts have for the machinery produced by Colin Seeley. A perfect example of imitation as the sincerest form of flattery.

While he may no longer build motorcycle frames, Colin Seeley has not turned his back on motorcycles, or even riding them. A Honda CB1100RD still gleams in his garage for gentle road use, or so he says, and anyone lucky enough to witness him demonstrating the URS 500 sidecar outfit, lovingly restored by a band of enthusiasts, would soon realise that his competitive spirit is very much alive.

Colin Seeley is likely to be active in motorcycling for a very long time. With his many skills and undoubted enthusiasm, who knows where? Or doing what? Watch this space is the intriguing order of the day.

CHAPTER 14

▮▮▮▮▮▮ *Segale*

Italy has always been known as the home of power-ful and beautiful automobiles. For many years, Luigi Segale has maintained that reputation in the world of motorcycling.

Luigi Segale entered the motorcycle business as a conventional motorcycle agent in 1972. However, within a comparatively short period of time, his talent for innovation and obvious engineering skills led to him carrying out conversions and modifications to series-production motorcycles, rendering them more suitable for competition in junior and national races.

The introduction of the F M 1 programme in 1979 meant that, in addition to national racing, there were international classes for T T 1–T T 2 and endurance events, which produced a demand for

suitable machines. This is the point at which Luigi Segale began the business for which he is now known to the motorcycling world.

As with many constructors, Luigi began by modi-fying production factory frames to improve per-formance, tailoring the modifications to suit each customer's needs. It was inevitable that eventually this would lead to the manufacture of complete frames or chassis for racing and sports use. Demand resulted in a small, but steady, production from this new constructor.

Segale took a major step in 1980 by exhibiting his work at the Bologna Motor Show. This paid divid-ends and resulted in several frames being built to house Honda, Kawasaki and Suzuki engines. Ver-sions of these machines were raced in F1 and F2 .

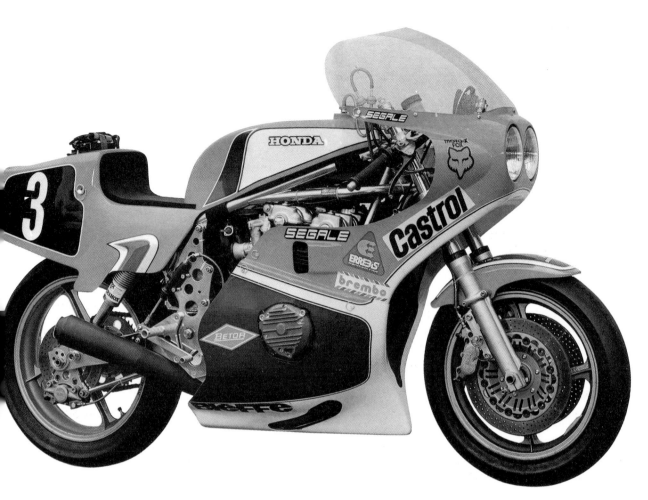

Left *This semi-monocoque, constructed from alloy honeycomb sandwich panels, is Segale's only departure from the use of steel tubing for motorcycle frames. The panels of the slab-sided structure were glued and riveted together to form a lightweight, yet very stiff, chassis. The engine was a 750 cc Ducati Desmo, its narrow layout making it ideal for this frame.*

Above *A Segale Honda 1000 endurance machine.*

Right *The Segale Honda 1000 in action.*

To capitalize on this new-found potential, and in an effort to turn out the best possible products, Luigi sought and found a top-class technician and welder with whom he could collaborate on the construction of the new designs. The man who filled this extremely important position was Austrian Dirk Ilderbrand.

The collaboration worked extremely well, Segale designing bikes (including all the bodywork), while Ilderbrand made the frames. However, in addition to a new range of successful racing and sports frames, Luigi Segale also began to offer a comprehensive engine building and tuning service. This was made available to established racing teams as well as the inevitable stream of private riders. Also

catered for were the riders of high-performance sports machines who wanted to improve the power output of their bikes' engines still further.

Since Segale's business was a Honda agency, the principal engines to receive the Segale treatment came from that manufacturer. However, this was by no means an exclusive arrangement, as Kawasaki and Suzuki engines were also modified by Segale.

During the Bologna Motor Show, the engineer Fabio Taglioni requested that Segale produce a special frame to house a 750 cc Ducati Desmo engine. The A. D. Elle engine was chosen, and was particularly suitable for the project because it was very narrow. The reason was because the frame for this

Above left The Segale Honda 954.

Left The frame construction of the 954. Note the use of the extended engine plates to carry both swinging fork pivots and shock absorber mount.

Above In this photograph of the 954, the quality of construction is evident, particularly the tube bending and welding.

machine was built utilizing composite materials.

The composite chassis was built from honeycomb sandwich panels. The complete load-bearing structure was assembled by gluing together the component parts with the assistance of some mechanical rivets. At the beginning of this project, problems were encountered in obtaining the aeronautical-type materials. However, with the co-operation of Signor Libanori of MV (who, as a matter of interest, was an MV rider in the 1950s and 1960s), and technical input from Signor Spairani, a director of SIAI Marchetti (part of the Agusta aeronautical group), this one-off composite chassis was completed.

As this special project was designed and built for Ducati, at the time of writing there was no performance data available, and the machine was still with Ducati in Bologna. However, this composite design does show the versatility and engineering capability of the Segale team.

Until this excursion into the use of composites, Segale frames had almost all been manufactured from CRO-MO steel tubing. In most cases, the engine would form a stressed member of the frame, that is the front section of the frame would be attached to the front of the engine at the bottom end of the front down-tube or tubes. Additional tubes would drop from the frame's top tube, or tubes, to the rear of the engine. These rear tubes would be attached to some plates, usually made from a material called Ergal 55. The plates formed attachments for the rear of the engine, and also the mounting and pivot for the rear suspension.

The swinging rear fork design used on almost all Segale frames is unique to them. It is based on a magnesium casting, made in a clay mould and machined to the required specification as a final stage. The underside of the rear fork is of open section with diagonal bracing ribs cast in. The combination of this open section and the use of magnesium provides a lightweight, but very strong, fork.

From the beginning, Segale frames have incorporated another important feature: a series of eccentric rings and special bearings that carry the steering head and provide an adjustable front fork angle, which means that the wheelbase can be changed quickly and easily. This can be of major importance during a race meeting. The feature is not exclusive to race frames, but is available on all of Segale's frames, allowing discerning sports riders to full advantage of it.

The front forks used on Segale frames are also of Segale's own design and manufacture. They have been in production since 1979, when Marzocchi could no longer supply forks to Segale's requirements. The forks were designed and manufactured in collaboration with the well-known engineer Enrico Ceriani, who was responsible for specifying the materials used. The cast magnesium legs and yokes, or trapezes, were the work of Luigi Segale himself.

The front forks have proved very successful for both race and road use. In fact, they have proved so

desirable that they were subsequently used, with various attachments, by the famous blue-blooded Italian Bimota company.

Originally, the rear suspension of Segale's machines utilized American Fox adjustable shock absorbers, which were claimed to be well made and light in weight. However, Segale eventually introduced his own progressive rear suspension, which only used Ceriani double-action shock absorbers.

During the early years of frame manufacture, Segale used the marvellous Campagnolo cast five-spoke wheels especially for racing. Then, during 1981, the notable technician Roberto Marchesini left Campagnolo to work for Betor Spagnolo (makers of forks and shock absorbers), where he was given the task of producing racing-type cast magnesium wheels to be marketed under the brand name of Betor.

At the Milan Motorcycle Show Marchesini offered the Betor wheels to Segale for Honda Italia's use in the world endurance championships and the Italian TT championship. In return for this generous offer, Segale gave Marchesini a design sketch of three-spoke cavity wheels, that is with hollow spokes.

Marchesini began producing these wheels in collaboration with the Marvic brand, but now offers them exclusively under the Marchesini label. All the bikes produced currently by Segale use these wheels. A satisfying outcome for all.

Up to and during 1980 Segale had produced many single or one-off machines, and to demonstrate the versatility of the designer, the models produced utilized many differing engine types. These included Ducati Desmo 750, Suzuki GSX550, Suzuki GSX750, Suzuki 1100R, Honda VF1000 and Honda CBX750.

Top A Kawasaki-based Segale, examples being available for 900, 1000 and 1100 cc engines.

Middle An F1 endurance machine built around a Suzuki 750 cc engine.

Left Another Segale Suzuki. This version can be supplied with a 750/1100 cc GSX engine or the 1000 cc TT1.

Right Mauro Rizzi in action in the Italian TT1 Championships, on the Segale 1000 cc Honda.

After a very successful 1980 season, Luigi Segale received a proposal from Dr Alcidei, the commercial director of Honda Italia, that he should become involved in the sport side at national level, in the TT1 category at junior level and in some international endurance races. Segale produced four machines for Honda Italia, who supplied two semi-official engines with spares. The remainder were supplied by Segale.

The following year, 1981, was a very positive one at the sportling level for Segale. Later that year, at the motorcycle show in Milan, he was to receive another important commission. This was from Dr Abbo, the Kawasaki importer, who wanted Segale to supply complete bikes less engines. These were to be sold to private buyers who wished to compete in TT1 or TT2.

Two examples of these Segale Kawasakis were exhibited on Kawasaki's stand at the Milan fair, and two were raced by Kawasaki Italia in the TT1 class that season. This Segale design worked extremely well, the machine winning three Italian championships: in 1982 and 1983 ridden by Roberto Suzzi, and in 1985 with Mauro Ricci.

During 1984 Segale entrusted one of the Kawasaki machines to a German rider, Tedesco Gerschewer, who had great success with it. Two other Kawasakis went to Germany, being purchased by Serge Rosset of Annemasse. They then went to private riders.

Following the success of the machines supplied to Honda Italia, Dr Alcidei commissioned four more machines from Segale, again to utilize engines supplied on a semi-official basis. These machines were to compete in the national and international endurance championships as well as the Italian TT1 championship.

To ensure that enough bikes and spares were available, Segale built eight machines. These were a great success at national level, winning the TT1 championship and the endurance championship. However, in the world endurance championship,

they were denied success, recording only a sixth place in Germany and a seventh place at Donnington, in England.

As well as the success enjoyed with Segale machines by the various importer teams, many private riders rode them to great effect. For example, during 1981, Segale supplied two French riders, Gherden and Ughen, with machines. These were fitted with Honda 1000 cc engines, and were used by the Frenchmen to seize second place in the Bol d'Or endurance race. They also achieved notable success in the world endurance championship as a private team. (Endurance racing has often proven to be a fine arena for privateers.)

For 1983 Honda Italia sold back to Segale the complete bikes, spares and tools originally supplied by him the season before. The price was attractive, but conditional on the bikes being raced at national level. To utilize these machines, Segale engaged the riding services of Mauro Ricci, of Bologna, and Roberto Suzzi of Imola.

Although both riders were experts in their category, a rivalry seemed to grow between them, and part way through the season Suzzi left to ride for Luigi Termignoni. Amazingly, his machine in the new team was a Segale Kawasaki, so Segale was still very well represented. In fact Suzzi finished in first place in the Italian T T 1 championship, while Ricci came third. So even with the loss of his team rider, Segale still won.

Apart from building sporting machines of the best quality for the discerning road user or sports rider, Luigi Segale has also produced many very successful racing bikes for a range of categories. Segale machines began competing in 1975–6. In the beginning, they were based on modified factory frames, the first being a Kawasaki 500 junior, followed by a 750 cc Kawasaki. During 1976 Segale modified his first Honda 500 cc junior, while 1977 was to see Segale gain his first positive result by winning the Italian national 500 cc championship. This was with a works-supplied machine, modified by Segale and ridden by Gianni Del Carro.

Another successful season followed in 1978, with second place in the Italian 500 cc championship using a modified Honda ridden by Angelo Laudati, and second place in the Italian 750 cc championship with a modified factory Kawasaki ridden by Marco Papa. In 1979 Angelo Laudati won the Italian championship for Segale on his modified 500 cc Honda, also the Italian junior championship with a modified Honda 500 cc. That year was also the first time that a full Segale Honda 954 was shown to the public, appearing at the Milan show.

Below left The Supermono 650 cc Segale Honda.

Right Although Luigi Segale has worked with machinery from several of the big manufacturers, 'Powered by Honda' has been the most prominent and successful signature on the fairing.

In 1980 the Segale Honda 954 made its race début, being ridden by Angelo Laudati and Gianni De Carro in the five-hour international race at Zandvoort. It came third, an amazing performance for a brand-new design. That year the bike also won the regional trophy with Angelo Laudati doing the riding. Segale won the regional trophy again in 1981 with a Honda 1000, the rider on this occasion being Walter Migliorati.

In the Italian endurance championship of 1982 a Segale machine came in first place, ridden by Angelo Laudati and Arturo Venanzi. In the 100-mile endurance race at Imola that year, Segale machines achieved second place, ridden by Maurizio Massuniani, and fourth place, ridden by Angelo Laudati. The machines were 1000 cc Segale Honda. Also in 1982 Roberto Suzzi won the Italian junior TT1 championship on a 1000 cc Segale Kawasaki.

A year later, Roberto Suzzi won the Italian TT1 championship on the 1000 cc Segale Kawasaki, while Mauro Rizzi finished third on a 1000 cc Segale Honda. In 1984 Vittorio Scatola finished in second place in the Italian TT1 championship on a 1000 cc Segale Honda.

Mauro Rizzi took a 1000 cc Segale Kawasaki to first place in the Italian Open championship of 1985. During that year the Segale business was transferred to its present site at 41 Galli Vigevano. At this point, Segale decided to give up his sporting activities to concentrate on the running of the agency, and on producing some special machines to exhibit at the Milan Show. These four specials utilized the Honda VF1000 engine. No new machines appeared in 1986, but in 1987 Segale designed and built another of his popular and exciting bikes. This utilized the Suzuki 1100R engine, and it was followed in 1989 by the first of the Supermonos, using the Dominator engine. The combination of this 650 cc Honda engine and the Segale machine that housed it was to have wide appeal. It became a limited-production machine from the Segale workshops. The popularity of Segale's workmanship, coupled with this exciting design, had led to exports to Japan, England and Germany.

In 1991 Segale produced yet another new model for the Milan Show. On this occasion, it was the Segale Honda CBR600RR, intended to offer the motorcycle world something exclusive, which it did quite effectively.

Trapeze artist

As this account shows, Luigi Segale and his partner Dirk Ilderbrand have given the motorcycling fraternity some very competitive race bikes and a continuing supply of exciting designs for the sporting road user. A reputation for top-quality build, using the best of materials, goes with the machines from the Segale workshop. Luigi Segale still feels that his task in life is to continue to offer his exciting bikes, built to his usual high standards, in limited numbers to discerning motorcyclists.

CHAPTER

15

■■■■■■ *Spondon Engineering*

The name Spondon Engineering needs absolutely no introduction to the motorcycle world. This famous independent frame builder has been producing racing and road frames for over 25 years. During this time, many makes and types of engine have been utilized. The company was formed in 1969 by Bob Stevenson and Stuart Tuller, both of whom had backgrounds that made them ideal candidates to run a business designing and building high-performance motorcycles.

Bob Stevenson had been an engineering apprentice with Rolls-Royce. This excellent training gave him the basic skills that were to become invaluable in his hobby and, later, his business. The hobby was motorcycle racing, which he participated in for 14 years; he was still racing during the early days of Spondon Engineering. During his racing career, Bob rode a variety of machines, including a BSA Gold Star, a 7R AJS and a road-racing 350 cc Greeves. On this last machine, he was able to win the club championship.

The other half of the Spondon partnership, Stuart Tuller, had spent his apprenticeship as an electrician with British Rail. This gave him a useful technical background for the new business. Like Bob, Stuart also rode racing motorcycles.

Valuable experience had been gained during their

racing years in carrying out modifications to their own machines to improve performance. This led to other riders asking them to make similar modifications to their machines. The demand for their services grew steadily until it became clear that there was the potential to build a business based on this work. As a result, Spondon Engineering came into being.

In the main, work for the newly-formed business consisted of making modifications to existing racing machines. These modifications were many and varied. They included producing different swinging rear forks, where it was felt that an improvement could be made on the standard factory parts; frames were modified to accept different engines, or to change the positions of other components, or quite often to increase stiffness. In many cases, where modifications were of a structural nature, engineering design was called for to achieve the required structural performance. This design work was to prove invaluable in the coming years.

Although they concentrated on modification work, the partners already had experience of building complete frames. In 1964 they had designed and built a steel-tubing frame to house a BSA Gold Star engine. This machine was unique in that the engine was laid flat to lower the centre of gravity. The bold and innovative design demonstrated the potential of the partnership, particularly when it is realized – as with several innovators in this book – that the work was carried out in a garden shed.

The next venture into frame building was with a machine built to house a Honda 125 cc engine. The completed machine was raced successfully by both Bob Stevenson and Stuart Tuller. This experience of 125 cc racing was to prove invaluable, as was the construction of that 125 racing frame. The first complete racing machine designed and built by Spondon Engineering, as a commercial enterprise, was a 125.

The first production machine was based on a steel-tubing frame, designed to house an AS1 Yamaha engine. Although produced for road use,

Above *The Barton-built 500 cc four-cylinder engine that was used in later Spartons. This machine was used as the basis for the Silver Dream Racer of film fame.*

Below *Bob Stevenson mounted on a 350 cc Greeves and competing at Skerries in Ireland in the late 1960s.*

Opposite *An example of the Sparton, built as a joint venture between Spondon Engineering and Barton Motors. The chassis housed the three-cylinder engine built by the latter.*

the engine proved both strong and turnable. In the Spondon frame, complete with a Spondon-designed swinging rear fork, it proved to be an affordable and very competitive package. So successful was it that over 120 examples were produced, which must be a record for a new company making only racing motorcycles.

The chassis design proved good enough to accept a larger 350 cc Yamaha engine. Once again, success on the track led to Spondon building over 15 of this version.

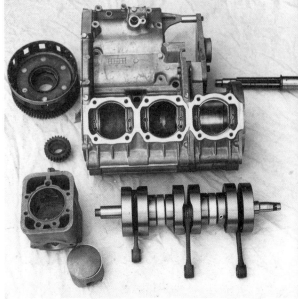

Above *This 1973 Spondon chassis was built to house a 500 cc twin-cylinder Suzuki.*

Opposite, below *In 1980 Spondon began building this type of racer. It was based on a 250 cc Rotax engine in a tubular steel frame.*

Below *The result of another joint venture, this time with engine builder Karef Zegers.*

Above *Karef Zegers' engineering skills are clearly demonstrated by these components. As can be seen, a new section has been grafted onto the crankcase of a twin-cylinder Yamaha TZ 350, while a new crankshaft and extra cylinder barrel have also been added. The result was a powerful three-cylinder two-stroke.*

Above right *A 1978 production run of tubular steel frames for the Yamaha E-type engine.*

SPONDON ENGINEERING

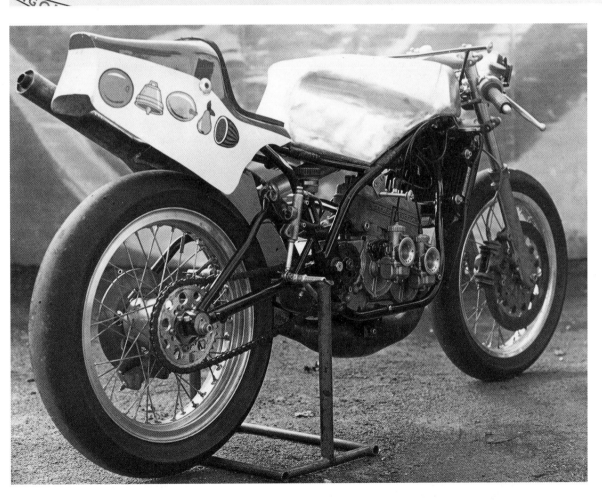

While the first production 125 cc machine was being produced, the usual one-offs and modifications, for which Spondon were renowned, were still being carried out. However, during the early 1970s, a bold and adventurous project was to be undertaken. This innovative move was put into operation by the forming of an alliance between Spondon Engineering and Barton Motors, the object being to produce a complete 500 cc racing machine.

The new machine was to be called the Sparton, a package that would be offered for sale by both companies involved. The unique aspect of this project was that Barton Motors were to produce the engine, while Spondon Engineering were to design and build the rolling chassis, and assemble the complete machine.

The engine for the Sparton was a hybrid, consisting of a 380 cc Suzuki crankcase to which were fitted specially-designed barrels. The result was a three-cylinder layout with a 500 cc capacity. It was housed in a steel-tubing frame, which featured a Spondon-designed swinging rear fork. The result was a competitive 500 cc racing machine.

Bob Stevenson raced a Sparton successfully him-

Above Clive Horton on a 250 cc Rotax-engined Spondon.

Above right A 1982 Spondon chassis with a 500 cc four-cylinder engine. Note that although this is a tubular frame, the tubing is of square section and is aluminium. This proved a significant step for the company in their design and construction of motorcycle frames.

Right Built during the early 1980s, this frame utilized steel tubing to house the four-cylinder Suzuki engine. The jig-welded method of construction is clear.

self. This attracted the attention of clubmen racers.

The Sparton was developed further when it received a completely new engine layout. Although the 500 cc capacity was retained, this later engine was of a square-four configuration. Again, the engine was built by Barton Motors. Over the next few seasons, between other work, the two companies built and sold 26 examples of the Sparton.

The early 1970s saw Spondon involved in another collaboration, in an effort to produce machinery that had the edge over the opposition. Again, the machine was to be of 500 cc capacity, and the

engine was to be a hybrid. The latter was a clever conversion by Karef Zegers, being based on the crankcase of the Yamaha T Z 350 cc twin-cylinder two-stroke. Another section of crankcase was grafted on, extending it to accept a third cylinder. Suitable cylinders were prepared and fitted, and a new crankshaft was produced. The result was a race-reliable, three-cylinder two-stroke engine.

The unique engine was housed in a Spondon designed and built steel tubing chassis. This machine was intended as an over-the-counter racer, and in this very competitive area attracted enough attention from club racers for 12 of them to be sold.

From the mid 1970s to 1980, Spondon were very busy in the production of replica frames. This work was centred on the E-type Yamaha engines of 250 and 350 cc capacity. The E-type had Yamaha's first mass-produced monoshock chassis.

The steel-tubing replica offered by Spondon Engineering proved so good that, over a few short seasons, 113 examples were produced. This work was interspersed with the production of one-off chassis – a service for which Spondon was, by then, renowned – and, of course, many modifications.

Above left *The Spondon twin-spar frame, constructed from extruded-alloy sections. In this case, the engine is a single-cylinder Rotax 500. The machine was built to race in the popular European Formula Single.*

Below left *A complete Spondon racer, powered by a 250 cc Rotax. Note the use of square-section alloy tubing. This type of construction was in use during 1983–4.*

Above *By 1988 Spondon were using alloy extrusions as a standard chassis material, as this four-cylinder Kawasaki example shows.*

The replica chassis produced by Spondon Engineering were very strong and also gave the machines excellent handling. As a result, the company's reputation grew, bringing in much more business.

The building of replica frames continued to be good business for Spondon with the production of a steel chassis to house the F G-type Yamaha engine. Again, the engine capacities were 250 and 350 cc. The popularity of this replica chassis was wide, and continued into the early eighties. During this period, 135 examples were produced.

Towards the end of the 1970s, the popularity of racing machines with larger-capacity engines was spreading. Spondon were able to take advantage of this by producing replica chassis to house the Yamaha T Z 750 cc engine. The production of replica frames was becoming an area for which Spondon Engineering had an excellent reputation, and it was to lead to further orders for this type of work.

At the beginning of the 1980s, Spondon were still producing replica chassis for the 350 cc Yamaha engine, but they had incorporated a major change. Although a replica in layout, the Spondon frame was now built from 2·5 cm (1 in) square alloy tubing. This move produced a chassis that gave the required structural performance, but showed a considerable weight saving over the steel-tubing version.

The use of alloy tube as a chassis material proved popular and successful. At first, these frames were only built for the 350 cc engines, but later 250 cc versions were also made. A measure of their potential was demonstrated when Martin Wimmer used one to win the 1982 British 250 cc Grand Prix. The popularity of Spondon's first alloy tube chassis was such that in just two seasons 30 examples were sold.

Although the use of 25 cm (1 in) alloy tubing for the frames was proving very successful, in their

usual effort to progress, Spondon began to introduce larger-section tubes. These were in extruded form and of commercial-grade alloy. This allowed them to produce frames that had improved structural performance.

Among the machines to gain advantage from the extruded alloy sections were some built for Dr Joe Erlich, of E M C fame. These were fitted with Rotax 250 cc engines. Although Spondon had built frames for E M C using the 25 cm (1 in) square tubing, the later versions took full advantage of the improvements offered by the extrusions and proved particularly successful. Over a period of time, Spondon produced 35 machines for Dr Erlich to race under the E M C banner.

Having seen the great advantages offered by the extruded alloy sections, both in ease of manufacture and the all-important improvements to structural performance, Spondon were to take this theme further. By the mid 1980s, they had optimized the use of alloy by the use of special extruded sections of their own design. They had financed the dies for the extrusions, ensuring that those designs remained exclusive to Spondon.

In the main, three extrusions were used, all rectangular in shape, but of different sizes. One aspect of the largest extrusion was that one corner was flattened. This particular extrusion was used for the main members of backbone or twin-spar frames, the flattened corner being positioned at the top. This gave the chassis a rounded-off appearance.

From a structural point of view, the larger sections of the extrusions automatically improved the bending stiffness and torsional performance of the frame members, but these qualities were further enhanced by integral longitudinal spars, or webs, inside the extrusions. In the largest section, two webs produced a cross-section that had the appearance of three square tubes joined together; the smaller extrusions each had a single web. The webs stabilized the outer walls when bending loads were applied to the extrusions, resisting any buckling. As a result, a far greater bending load was required to force the extrusion walls to buckle.

Thus, without changing the outside dimensions of the extrusion, the stiffness was greatly improved. The overall performance and quality of these extrusions were further enhanced by the use of the higher-grade 7020 alloy.

The use of these specialized extrusions has since become Spondon's standard method of frame construction. Backbone or twin-spar chassis would have the largest extrusion as the backbone or spars, while the smaller-section extrusions, would form

Left *This 1991 Spondon frame shows the use of a wider range of extrusion sizes. It also demonstrates the excellent overall design and finish that has come to be expected from the company's road bikes.*

Above *In 1991 Spondon were still producing replica chassis, as this 250 cc Yamaha B racer shows.*

Below *This frame was designed to cope with a high-performance powerplant, being intended for a road bike based on a turbocharged, four-cylinder Suzuki engine.*

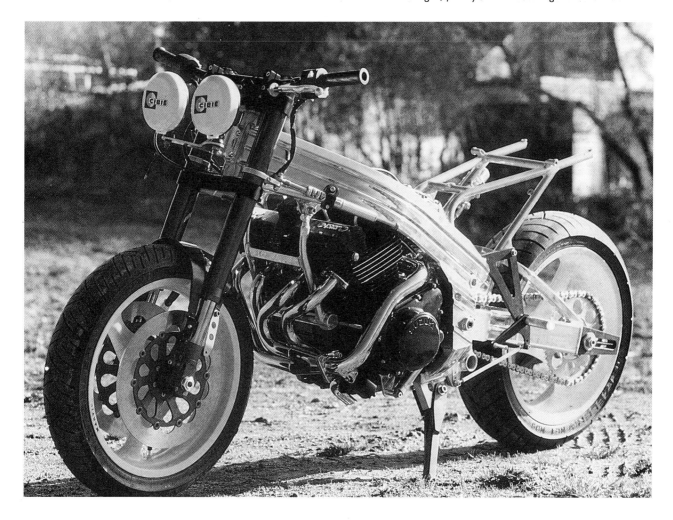

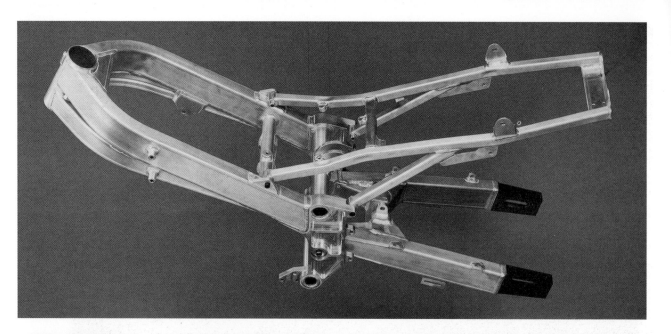

the remainder: engine mounts, sub-frames for seat, etc. Another advantage of using this variety of extrusions is that Spondon have been able to utilize them in another structural application: the highly-stressed swinging rear fork.

Extrusions lend themselves to being bent and welded, and because of the latter, more than one size or type of extrusion can be used in the same structure. In addition, load-bearing points, engine mounts, chain adjusters, etc, are all easily incorporated, making this type of construction very versatile from both the structural and production aspects.

During the 1980s, Spondon were to widen their horizons and enter new markets. In the beginning, they had used their experience and expertise to produce a very wide range of racing machines, but this new era was to see them beginning to design and manufacture road bikes.

Spondon were able to offer the road bike customer a special service, that is the entire machine could be tailored to meet the customer's requirements. This included the choice of engine. In most cases, the engine was of a large capacity, and could be of almost any make or type. As time went by, the company built road bikes around most of the popular suitable engines.

The road bike business became a significant part of Spondon Engineering's production, and to enhance this aspect, they began to build road bikes of their own design, based on popular engines. These were offered for sale 'off-the-shelf'.

Above left The production Norton F1 chassis. Spondon
built 200 of these, the machines being assembled by Norton
themselves.

Left A good example of Spondon's frame work. This design
utilizes several different sizes of alloy extrusion, as well as
machined sections to connect the lower ends of the twin
spars to the rear swinging fork pivot. A Yamaha 750 cc twin
completes this racing machine.

Above Where it all started – the production of racing
machines. Brian Reid is shown mounted on a Spondon-built
350 cc Yamaha, just one of many.

Although road bikes were a major business for
Spondon during the eighties, they still produced a
considerable number of racing machines. Their output of complete machines was made up of approximately 75 per cent road bikes and 25 per cent
racing bikes.

During 1990, Spondon were contracted by Norton to produce the chassis for the new F1 road bike.
This was of the twin-spar type and made full use of
alloy extrusions. It was designed to house Norton's
new rotary engine.

Spondon supplied the complete chassis, which
included the swinging rear fork and sub-frame,
while Norton completed the assembly. This was a
significant step for Spondon, as they had to produce

200 complete chassis to meet the homologation
requirements so that the machine could be classi-
fied as a production bike for racing purposes.

As well as fulfilling the Norton contract, Spondon Engineering also designed and built a series of
machines for a Far Eastern customer. While these
production runs were being carried out, the one-
offs and specials continued to be built. These were
of varied and interesting designs. An impressive
machine is currently taking shape, the Spondon-
designed chassis housing a turbocharged engine.

Attention to detail

The ability, experience and enthusiasm that lie
behind Spondon Engineering are all reasons why
such a wide variety of excellent road and racing
machines have come from this factory. Many
famous names have been customers, among them
the legendary (what else!) Barry Sheene.

Their devotion of equal attention and expertise to
a single chassis as to a production run has been
instrumental in the company's success, from both
technical and commercial points of view. Moreover,
a move to a large, well-equipped factory facility is
an indication that Spondon Engineering intend to
continue designing and building the types of motorcycle chassis for which they are famous for many
years to come.

▮▮▮▮▮▮ Overview

As this book shows, the independent motorcycle designers and builders have played a very important part in the development and production of motorcycles, for both road and race use. To gain, and retain, their commercial positions, they continually strive to advance technology, and because of their independence are often able to bring new innovations into use much more quickly than the major manufacturers. In addition, they are often better suited to producing small numbers of a particular design, which explains some of the very exotic, limited-edition machines that are produced by the independents.

Independent motorcycle designers and builders may be associated with very small companies or large, well-financed organizations. This, of course, results in some having far more extensive facilities than others which, in turn, may have some effect on the company's capability. In most cases, however, this relates to quantity rather than quality. The companies covered by this book range from the small to the large, some of whom are current producers of motorcycles, while others are no longer in production. However, all have contributed to the advancement of motorcycle technology and engineering, and in most cases have been commercial successes.

Of course, they are only some of the many independent companies and individuals who have contributed to the progress of motorcycle design, but they are typical of the talent that exists in this fascinating and exciting world. It would be impossible to include all the independent motorcycle frame makers in one book, and to those who have made a contribution to this aspect of motorcycling, but are not mentioned, the author apologises.

We end this book with some illustrations of the recent work of the independents, as a reminder that their day is far from over.

Opposite, above 1995 Bimoto Supemono, powered by BMW. (Photo: Phil Masters).

Opposite, below What Bakker did to the Harley-Davidson, in 1994. (Photo: Roland Brown).

Above right A 1993 Magni Australia with 1000cc Guzzi engine; (Photo: Oli Tennent).

Top *1993 Segale SR 900, 1993. (Photo: Oli Tennent).*

Right *An Egli transformation of the Harley-Davidson, 'Lucifer's Hammer', 1993. (Photo: Oli Tennent).*

Below *A PDQ Battlemax prototype, 1994. (Photo: Roland Brown).*